+

Typography 21
The Annual of the TypeDirectorsClub

TDC 46• P.000

Adult dosage
The construction of this book should be undertaken
with precautionary measures. Our medium can provoke
a workable read with relaxing intervals.

Can be viewed 3-4 times daily for a period of 3 months.
If symptoms persist consult your doctor.

+

Typography 21
The Annual of the TypeDirectorsClub

TDC 46+ P.001

— — —   —

QUALITY ASSURED

CONTENTS: The highest quality typographical work.

Information: The design of this product is intended to aid navigation of the work within.
Crafted with pride. ©2000 ATTIK.

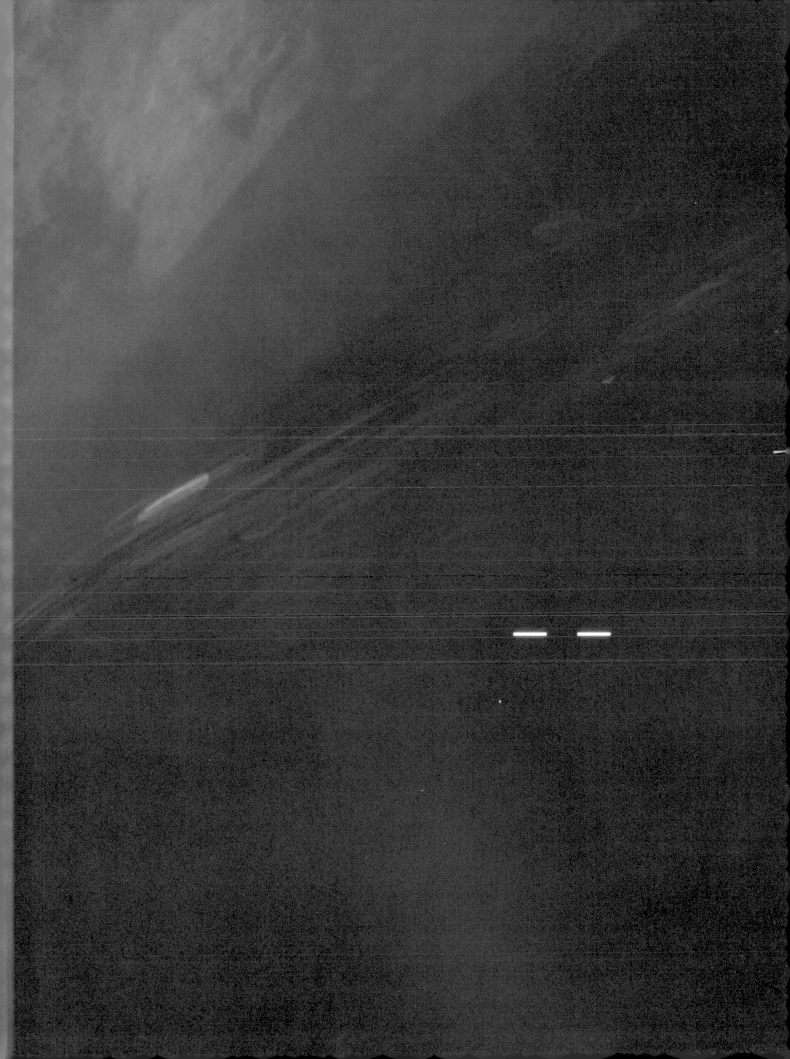

TypeDirectorsClub
Acknowledgements

TDC 46+ P.004

First published in 2000 in the
United States by HBI, an imprint of
HarperCollins Publishers, Inc.
10 East 53rd Street
New York, NY 10022-5299

Distributed in the U.S. and Canada
by Watson-Guptill Publications
770 Broadway
New York, NY 10003-9595
ISBN 0-8230-5555-8

Distributed throughout
the rest of the world by
HarperCollins International
10 East 53rd Street
New York, NY 10022-5299
Fax: 212-207-7654

ISBN 0-06-019892-3

The Library of Congress
has cataloged this serial title
as follows:
Typography
(Type Directors Club (U.S.)}
Typography: The Annual of the
Type Directors Club.
New York:HBI
2000

Annual.

Typography (New York, NY)
1. Printing, Practical—Periodicals.
2. Graphic arts—periodicals.
3. Type Directors Club (U.S.)

Printed in Hong Kong by
Everbest Printing Co. Ltd.
through Four Colour Imports, Ltd.,
Louisville, Kentucky
Color Origination: Classicscan Pte
Ltd (Singapore)
Paper: 128gsm Korean Matt Art

Acknowledgments
The Type Directors Club gratefully
acknowledges the following for
their support and contributions
to the success of TDC46 and
TDC³ 2000:

Design & A/W: ATTIK
Aporva Baxi, Simon Dixon,
Paul Driver, John O'Callaghan,
David Rothblatt, Michael Spoljaric

Exhibition Facilities:
The Aronson Galleries,
Parsons School of Design
Judging Facilities: School of Visual Arts
Chairpersons and Judges' Photos:
Fran Collins

TDC46 Competition
(call for entries):

Design: ATTIK. Paul Driver

Printer: The Hennegan Press
Paper: Fox River Paper Co.

TDC² 2000 Competition
(call for entries):
Design: Linda Florio Design
Printer: Printing Methods, Inc.
Prepress: A to A Graphic Services, Inc.
Paper: Potlatch 70# Mountie Matte

The principal typeface used in the
composition of TYPOGRAPHY 21
Akzidenz Grotesk BE.

Contents

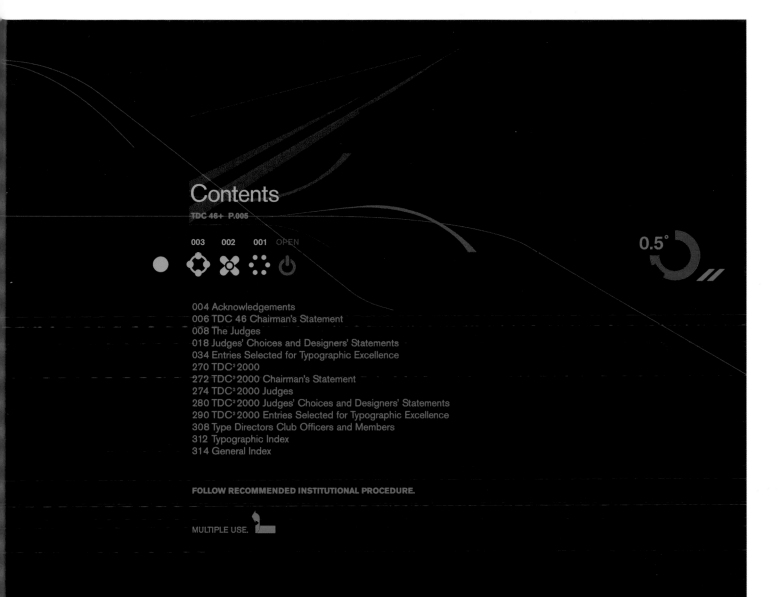

003   002   001   OPEN

004 Acknowledgements
006 TDC 46 Chairman's Statement
008 The Judges
018 Judges' Choices and Designers' Statements
034 Entries Selected for Typographic Excellence
270 TDC² 2000
272 TDC² 2000 Chairman's Statement
274 TDC² 2000 Judges
280 TDC² 2000 Judges' Choices and Designers' Statements
290 TDC² 2000 Entries Selected for Typographic Excellence
308 Type Directors Club Officers and Members
312 Typographic Index
314 General Index

FOLLOW RECOMMENDED INSTITUTIONAL PROCEDURE.

MULTIPLE USE.

when a word crosses the line, it becomes invincible

+

TypeDirectorsClub
Chairman's Statement

TDC 46+ P.006

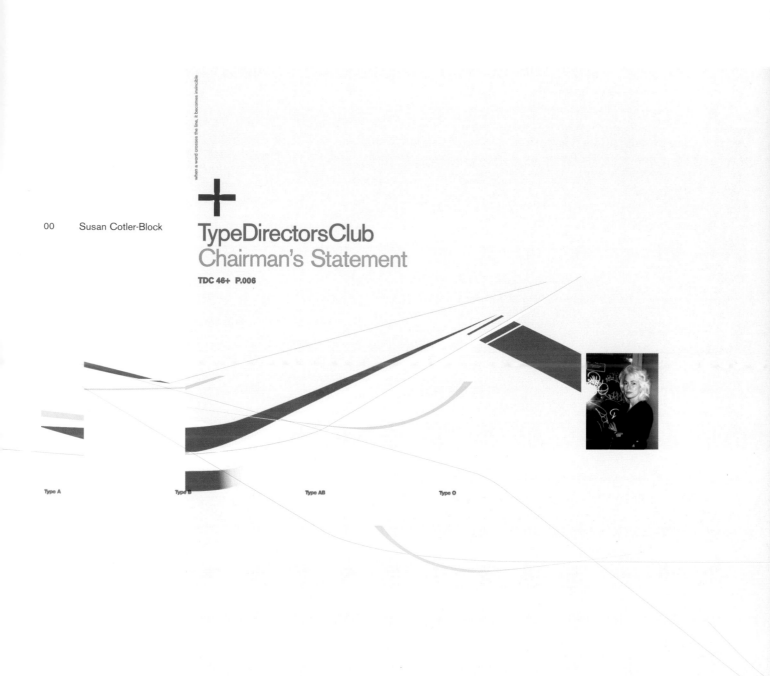

Type A   Type B   Type AB   Type O

To judge the 3,346 entries (from 33 countries) for TDC 46 and choose the winners for this competition, I selected a diverse team of judges whose work, for me, represents the standard by which typographic excellence should be measured. The judges were Bridget DeSocio, David Ellis, Chip Kidd, Lana Rigsby, Ina Saltz, James Sommerville and Anthony Vagnoni. I want to thank them all. The entrants for their entries, ATTIK for the design of the call, invitations, posters, certificates and annual, and the judges for throwing themselves into the task at hand, and though it was a daunting task, managing to maintain their high level of enthusiasm throughout a grueling two days of judging. The outcome seen here is a wondrous panorama, which chronicles the best of the best typographic design produced in the last year of the 20th century. These winning entries mark the end of an incredible era. Looking back on the 20th century, we see some amazing technological advances. My 89 year-old mother-in-law, who was born long before the invention of television, is so busy these days emailing everyone she knows, that she hardly has the time anymore, to spend on spinning wool (she no longer dyes her own), and knitting baby booties. She has essentially traded in her spinning wheel and knitting needles for her laptop! It truly is a "Brave New World". As we enter the new millennium, we do so with all the excitement and trepidation that is always created by a journey into the unknown. And, as an educator, I can only hope that this superb collection of typographic excellence will inspire the growth of future generations of designers, well into the 21st century.

Susan Cotler-Block is Chair of the Advertising Design Department (which includes Graphic and Packaging Design) at the Fashion Institute of Technology. She joined the faculty in 1977. Susan counts amongst her many accomplishments, the design of the current course in Publication Design (Magazine Editorial/Layout) in the BFA Program of the Advertising Design Department, and chairing the Advertising Design Department's Academic Standards Committee. Also, as a member of the Advertising Design Department's Curriculum Committee, Susan has been instrumental in shaping the AD/BFA program, by pioneering interdisciplinary assignments between the Photography, Illustration, and Advertising Design departments, adding Typography to the curriculum of the Foundation Year of the AD/AAS Degree program, and adding Web Design to the curriculum of the AD/BFA Degree Programs. Susan is currently adding an Evening/Weekend AD/BFA Degree program to FIT's many offerings. This program is scheduled to begin Fall 2000, and will afford working people the opportunity for higher education in the field of Graphic Design. A graduate of the School of Visual Arts, and the recipient of a full tuition scholarship from the School Art League, Susan has provided art direction for such organizations as Family Communications, Sterling Publications, Avon, MacFadden Bartell, Book-of-the-Month Club, the New York Health and Racquet Club, Hearst Publishing, Watson-Guptill, Ziff Davis, the Pablo Picasso Society, and the Erté Society. Susan is also the principal of Circle, Square and Triangle Graphic Designs, Inc., a niche advertising agency, specializing in print media. Currently, Susan is a member of the Board of Directors of the Type Directors Club and Chair of their Scholarship Committee. She is also a member of the New York Art Directors Club, the Society of Publication Designers, the Society of Illustrators, and the American Institute of Graphic Arts. Susan consistently introduces her students to the benefits of professional club membership through student attendance at speaker lectures and seminars. "Bringing student and industry together early on in the academic process, through professional societies and clubs, benefits everyone." In addition, Susan is a Fine Artist and has had her paintings shown in New York and London.

Biography
Statement

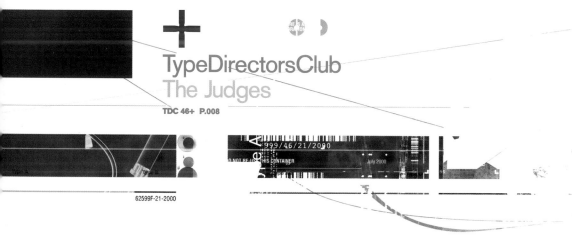

TypeDirectorsClub
The Judges

62599F-21-2000

OBJECTIVITY GUARANTEED

SECTION CONTAINS: 7 Judges' Biographies and Sample Work.
Judges: Bridget DeSocio David Ellis Chip Kidd Lana Rigsby
Ina Saltz James Sommerville Anthony Vagnoni

J.01   Bridget DeSocio   Socio X
New York

J.02   David Ellis   Why Not Associates
London

J.03   Chip Kidd   Chip Kidd Design
New York

\#   Name   Company
Location

Art Director of Extremes has a passion for the visual culture in all its varied forms from *PAPER Magazine* to *Town & Country* or Cone Denim to Vera Wang. More than simply a graphic designer, Bridget's interest in the meaning of the signs and symbols that surround us makes her a cultural critic extraordinaire. DeSocio bills herself not as a graphic designer, which she is by trade, but as a semiologist, motivating desire, studying the commercial why. Fueled by social purpose, DeSocio is a designer manqué. Her clients are paying her as much for her Toffler instincts as for her trademark tech-with-taste work. "We get approached by people who want to take a new look at the classics as well as a classic look at the new." Socio X, the three-year-old design firm in New York, founded by Bridget DeSocio, boasts an impressive client roster, which includes cultural icons such as Kodak, Palm Pilot, Vera Wang, Cone Denim, Pantone, *PAPER Magazine*, *Town & Country* Magazine, Saks Fifth Avenue, David Byrne, Island Records, Rizzoli and Hermés. In just a short time Socio X has gained international attention and praise from design industry institutions such as The New York Art Directors Club, Type Directors Club, Society of Publication Designers, *Communication Arts Magazine* and *Print Magazine*. *ID Magazine* and *Graphis Magazine* have both ranked the firm among the top ten in the design field. Her work has been exhibited by the Cooper-Hewitt Museum, and twice included in the New York Art Directors Club's YOUNG GUNS exhibition. She has been an influence to sub-culture kids, skate culture and gen Xers for over ten years as a result of her on-going relationship as Creative Director of New York City's *PAPER Magazine* (consistently known for its ever-changing logo, which has never appeared the same twice).

David Ellis set up Why Not Associates with Andrew Altmann after graduation from the Royal College of Art in 1987. Since then they have lectured in England, Germany, France, Holland, Switzerland, Japan, America, and Australia. They have designed exhibition material for various clients including the ICA, the Foreign and Commonwealth Office, Pompidou Centre, Royal Academy of Arts, Natural History Museum, and the DTI, and have designed postage stamps and booklets for the Royal Mail. Why Not Associates directed television and film titles including a ppb [what's that? "paid political broadcast," maybe?] for the Labour Party shortly before the last election. They produced two , three , & four dimensional work for clients including Antony Gormley, the Barbican Centre, One Telecom, Branson Coates, Virgin Records, Chiat/Day, Adidas, BBC, Bellsouth, Branson Coates Architecture, British Telecom, Channel 4, the Design Museum, the Green Party, *Shots* magazine, Hull City Council, the ICA, Internos Books, Kobe Fashion Museum, Lancaster City Council, Midland Bank, the Next Directory, Oilily, the Royal Academy of Arts, Renault, Smirnoff, *Time* magazine, *Upper and lowercase* magazine, and Weiden & Kennedy. David Ellis has fathered several children. [Or does he mean that why not, collectively, have fathered several children? Originally it was just "Fathered several children," which is completely ambiguous. You'll have to ask him. If it's they, collectively, then say, "Why Not Associates have..." and begin the next sentence, "David Ellis is currently designing:..."] He is currently designing: a 000-metre typographic pavement of bird literature in Morecambe, a book for architect Nigel Coates, Euro 2000 films for Nike, and an e-commerce issue of *Time* magazine.

A graphic designer and writer in New York City. His book jacket designs for Alfred A. Knopf (where he has worked for over thirteen years) have helped spawn a revolution in the art of American book packaging. His work has been featured in *Vanity Fair*, The Graphic Edge (by Rick Poyner), *Eye*, *Print* (cover story), *Entertainment Weekly*, *The New Republic*, *Time*, *The New York Times*, *Graphis*, *New York* and *ID* magazine. The latter chose him as part of its first *ID* 40 group of the nation's top designers and has awarded him "Best of Category, Packaging" twice. In 1997, he received the International Center of Photography's award for Use of Photography in Graphic Design, and he is a regular contributor of visual commentary to the Op-Ed page of *The New York Times*. In 1998, he was made a member of the Alliance Graphique Internationale (AGI). His designs have been described as "monstrously ugly" (John Updike), "apparently obvious" (William Boyd), "faithful flat-earth rendering" (Don DeLillo), "surprisingly elegant" (A.S. Mehta), "a distinguished parochial comic balding Episcopal priest" (Allan Gurganus), "two colors plus a sash" (Martin Amis), and "not a piece of hype. My book was lucky." (Robert Hughes). Mr. Kidd has also written about graphic design and popular culture for *Vogue*, *The New York Observer*, *Entertainment Weekly*, *Details*, *2WICE*, *The New York Post*, *ID* and *Print*. He has authored Batman Collected (Bulfinch, 1996), in which he attempts to rid himself of his inner demons. To no avail—he is co-author and designer of the subsequent Batman Animated (HarperCollins, Fall 1998).

J.01   J.02   J.03

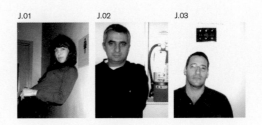

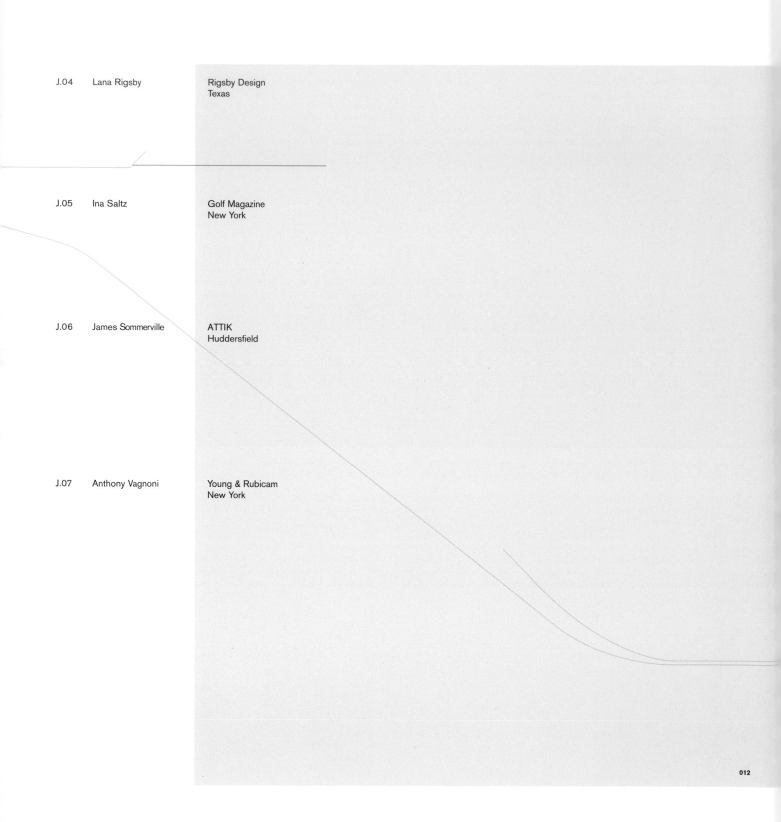

J.04   Lana Rigsby   Rigsby Design
                             Texas

J.05   Ina Saltz   Golf Magazine
                             New York

J.06   James Sommerville   ATTIK
                             Huddersfield

J.07   Anthony Vagnoni   Young & Rubicam
                             New York

Name   Company
                             Location

Lana Rigsby is principal of Rigsby Design, a Texas-based firm known for creating engaging, intelligent communications for a diversity of organizations. Her firm's work includes branding, corporate identity, and web site development for such companies as Dell Computers, Weyerhaeuser, Mohawk Paper Mills, American Oncology Resources, and the Earth Technology Corporation. Rigsby has edited and designed three comprehensive volumes on annual-report design: Graphis International Annual Reports volumes 5, 6, and 7. She co-chaired the AIGA's 1998 business conference, Brandesign. Her work has been consistently recognized in the most respected national and international design forums, including Communication Arts, Graphis, the New York Art Directors Club, the AIGA, and the Type Directors Club; it is included in the Cooper-Hewitt National Design Museum's exhibition "Mixing Messages: Graphic Design in Contemporary Culture." Lana has lectured on design throughout the U.S., and serves as a national director for the American Institute of Graphic Arts.

Ina Saltz is the Design Director of Golf Magazine which has a circulation of 1.5 million. Ina has previously art-directed Time magazine's International Edition, Worth, Golf for Women, Worldbusiness, PC Tech Journal, High School Sports, and Home Video magazines; she has been a consulting art director at Business Week and The New York Times Magazine; her redesign projects include the Dow Jones Investment and the Hamilton Alumni Review. Ina was one of the first art directors to work on a computer, in 1981, where she created animated graphics as part of Time Inc.'s Teletext Project, a precursor of the World Wide Web. She is a member of the design faculty of the Stanford Professional Publishing Course and a member of the board of the Type Directors Club as well as of the Society of Publication Designers. Ina graduated from the Cooper Union for the Advancement of Science and Art in New York City, where she studied painting and calligraphy. She is on the Alumni Council at Cooper Union, and she completed several terms on its Executive Board.

James Sommerville [Hon DLitt], co-founder of ATTIK, was born and raised in the North of England in Huddersfield, West Yorkshire. After graduating from Batley Art and Film School, he opened a graphic design studio at age 19 in his grandma's attic bedroom, with college friend Simon Needham. Since then, James has been a major force in positioning ATTIK as one of the world's most innovative group of people, now with further offices in London, New York, San Francisco and Sydney. In his drive to push new avenues of business and creativity, James developed creative solutions for local, regional and national brands, established himself as a commercial director and filmed a short documentary—Negative Forces, Witchcraft and Idolatry. As well as continuing to direct, James now takes on the global role of overseeing the development of ATTIK's strategic brand and business positioning throughout all five offices. Recently, James sat on the panel of the 'Labour Government Internet Inquiry' and has been requested by HRH The Prince of Wales Trust to become an advisor to The Princes' Youth Business Trust. James and ATTIK have also been awarded the BACC Transatlantic Entrepreneurial Business Award 2000 for their outstanding contributions to strengthening the vital economic relationship between the UK and US. This year, the University of Huddersfield presented James with the Degree of Honorary Doctor of Letters to formally recognize an 'outstanding global creative business success'.

Anthony Vagnoni is the publicity director for creative work at Young & Rubicam Inc. In this role he is responsible for raising the profile of the creative work of the various Y&R companies. Prior to joining Y&R in January of 2000, he was an editor at large for Advertising Age, where he covered a wide range of issues and trends that affected advertising and marketing. He joined Ad Age in September of 1997 from Creativity magazine, Ad Age's glossy publication devoted to examining the best new creative work in print and broadcast advertising. Anthony joined Creativity in 1990 as managing editor, and was named editor the following year. A native of Washington, D.C., Anthony graduated from New York University with a Bachelor of Fine Arts degree in film and television. He lives a pastoral life in the Jersey suburbs with his two young daughters.

J.04   J.05   J.06   J.07

+

J.01   Bridget DeSocio
J.02   David Ellis
J.03   Chip Kidd

TypeDirectorsClub
Judges' Work

TDC 46+ P.014

MULTIPLE VIEWING RECOMMENDED.

J.04   Lana Rigsby
J.05   Ina Saltz
J.06   James Sommerville
J.07   Anthony Vagnoni

+

TypeDirectorsClub
Judges' Work

TDC 46+ P.016

J.04

J.05

EXTRA SECTION: The Top 25 Golf Schools

GOLF
MAGAZINE.

NEW RESEARCH:
WHERE
YOU MISS
WHY
YOU MISS
AND WHAT TO
DO ABOUT IT

MORE INSTRUCTION: on chipping,
putting, swing speed, and power
PLUS 5 PRIVATE LESSONS

J.06

Negative Forces, Witchcraft and Idolatry

J.07

creativity

TypeDirectorsClub
The Judges' Choices and Designers' Statements
TDC 46+ P.018

QUALITY ASSURED

SECTION CONTAINS: 7 Judges' Choices, Work and Statements.

Judges Choices: Bridget DeSocio/Bill Cahan David Ellis/Antje Hedde Chip Kidd/B.J. Krivanek
Lana Rigsby/Design: M/W Ina Saltz/Werner Schneider James Sommerville/Jennifer Sterling
Anthony Vagnoni/Bill Douglas

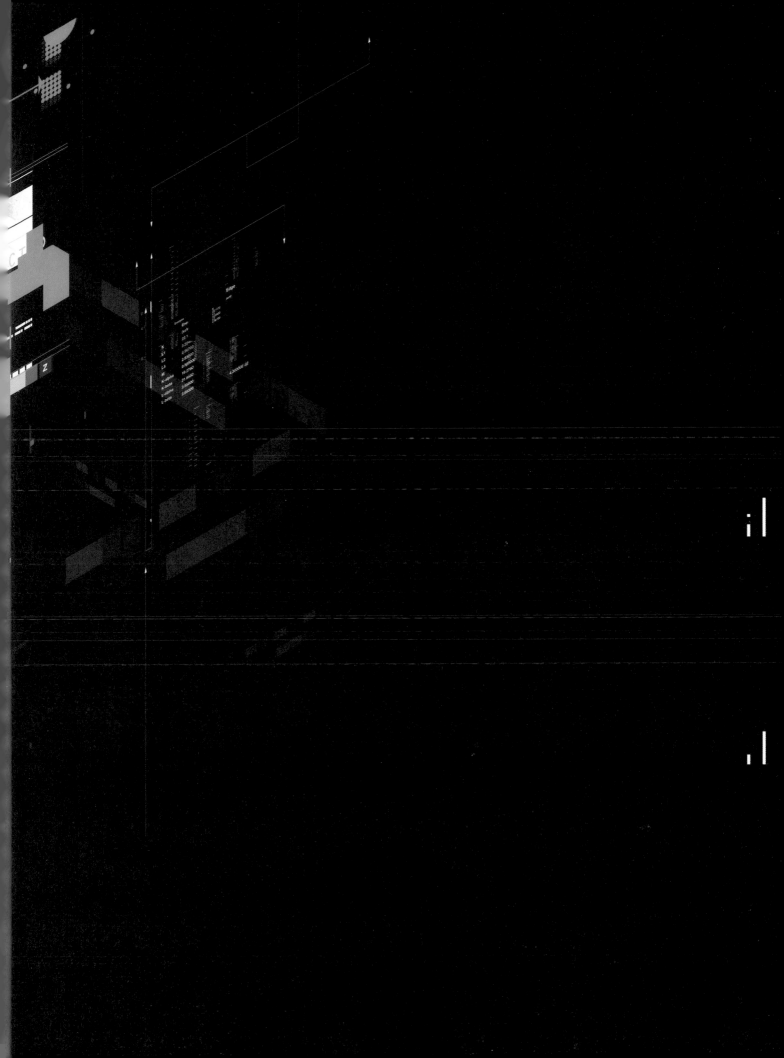

Annual Report

Design_Bob Dinetz,
San Francisco, California
Art Direction_Bill Cahan

Creative Direction_Bill Cahan
Copywriters_Thom Elkjer and
Bob Dinetz
Design Office_Cahan & Associates
Client_General Magic

Principal Type_Akzidenz Grotesk   **Dimensions**_5½ x 7½ in. (14 x 19.1 cm)

J.01   Bridget DeSocio

D.01.5   Bill Cahan

\#   Name

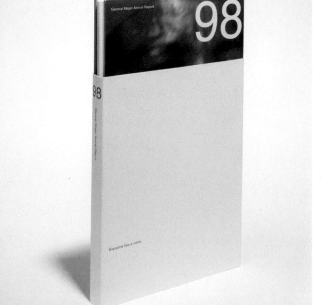

AUDIOVISUAL and MULTILINGUAL. If talk is type in the auditory realm. This piece's plain and simple use of words streaming across the mouths of multi-culti heads all aligned on a fold out format ~50 feet long says so much about what type means deeply. It means sound in the mouth and it means language to the eye and it means interaction. Today it ALSO means global communication in a non-language-specific way. This piece is not about fonts, nor is it about surface materials, e.g., paper, printing inks, or spot varnishes. It is about a world-wide commonality, intuitive communication, speech enabling technology and a non-linguistic-dependent interface. I am not implying that typography is passé or that intuitive computing via speech enabling technology is what is NOW, I am merely saying that a great piece is intuitively made and formed from a direct, languageless approach to design. You should understand the content without having to search for the subtext... A great piece of typography works without language, just as computing will eventually work without a keyboard.

Though General Magic has unique technologies and interesting products, what seemed most compelling was simply the idea of your own voice being the next interface with the digital environment. Ironically, people have always tried to control their televisions, cars and computers by speaking to them. Now, General Magic wants to make the human voice the logical replacement for the graphical user interface (GUI). We made a case for voice as the most natural way to communicate throughout the world. Rather than confine the message to a narrow application or product, it was this broad idea that would be associated with General Magic.

Book

Design_Antje Hedde,
London, England
Lettering_Antje Hedde
Art Direction_Antje Hedde

Creative Direction_Kurt Georg
Dieckert and Stefan Schmidt
Photography_Julian Broad,
Colin Gray, Mischa Haller,
Martin Parr and Terry Richardson
Agency_Springer & Jacoby
International, London
Client_DaimlerChrysler AG

Principal Type_Various

Dimensions_5 $^{15}/_{16}$ x 8 ¼ in. (15 x 21 cm)

J.02   David Ellis

D.02.5   Antje Hedde

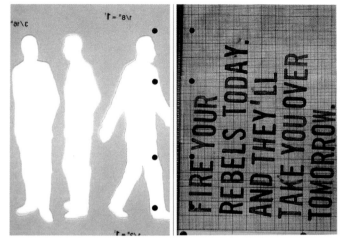

Every year there is a lot of great work entered for the Type Directors Club awards, and this year is no exception. However, within all that excellence there are occasional pieces that really make me excited. And what they have in common is that they have broken out of their market definitions. This takes balls. There are many examples of thought-provoking, cutting-edge new design on show this year, but not many of them are for such a mainstream blue-chip company as Mercedes-Benz. Hats off to Antje Hedde at Springer & Jacoby for the book to mark the launch of the Mercedes A-class. Not many people would even attempt to produce such an arresting design for this kind of client. Most designers would assume that contemporary design, utilitarian binding techniques, edgy typography, and oblique imagery would be outside the realm acceptable to Mercedes-Benz. For me, this book is a million times more adventurous and exciting than any style magazine or music CD package you care to mention. Top notch.

Our lives are guided by so many rules that external pressures constrict our way of thinking. But who's to say that a room should have four walls, that a bicycle should have two wheels, that a Mercedes should always look like a Mercedes? This is exactly the reason why the founders of the car built the A-class. It is the result of a new thinking generation. Whilst the A-class was being developed, S&J also had to devise a new method of communication, which meant breaking with convention and has resulted in the production of this book, showing the thoughts of a new generation. These thoughts are presented typographically with items taken from a sub-culture which the new generation come into contact within everyday life. The use of grey as a background colour on the right page is still a link to Mercedes-Benz CI. This book has been written and designed for those who do not want to be part of the mainstream.

Outdoor Environment

Design_Community Architexts,
Chicago, Illinois
Art Direction_B.J. Krivanek

Photography_Edward Lines, Jr.
Witnesses and Writers_Halyna
Boyko-Hrushetsky, Ivan Kolomayets,
Lydia Kurylak, Lena Schrebetz-
Skyba, and Sinovi Turkalo
Program Director_Jennifer
Van Winkle
Design Assistant_Cynthia Perkin
Researcher_Karla Roberts

Principal Type_Futura Heavy and
Matrix Bold

Funders_Chicago Department
of Cultural Affairs,
Gaylord & Dorothy Donnelley
Foundation, and Illinois Arts Council

J.03   Chip Kidd

D.03.5   B.J. Krivanek

Name

 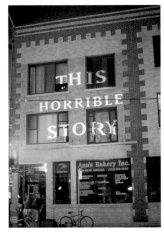  

In the interest of full disclosure, I have to say: for me it was a toss-up between two outstanding entries. The commercial for Tide detergent by Imaginary Forces (which I assume is elsewhere in this tome—check it out) is truly astonishing on more than one level: it's not only technically masterful in a way I've never before seen; it's original, ground-breaking work commissioned by, of all people, Proctor and Gamble (!). Just picturing what the agency must have gone through to get it approved makes me want to weep openly, and at the same time gives me a vicarious sense of hope. The other submission that I kept returning to is called "Witnesses," a project out of California State University that explored the experiences of local Ukrainian village survivors of the 1932–33 Ukrainian

famine, and compared them to those of today's suburban Chicago schoolchildren. Statements were taken from both parties, typeset (handsome, bold, blocky Futura—readable on any surface), and projected onto buildings that faced each other across a campus street. The result was a conversation that spanned space and time as dramatically as it spanned generations, and all on a scale that was truly impossible to ignore. Ultimately, I had to cast a blind eye to Form and base my decision on Content. That is: I ignored what the typography of both looked like and let their words speak to me. That is after all, what type is for. After that it was easy—"Learn from History" vs. "Buy more Tide." No contest.

This multi-disciplinary site activation involved the projection of large-scale texts onto two buildings which face each other across Chicago Avenue. These dynamic, historic billboards suggest a dialogue between factions in the Ukrainian Village community—elderly survivors of the 1932-33 Ukrainian Famine (Us) and outsiders such as Soviet officials and recent Latino immigrants (Them) represented by the voices of Soviet propaganda and local Chicago

schoolchildren. This site work explored the commodification of land, crops, labor, real estate, and history itself, while drawing parallels between the historic genocide and the contentious survival of urban children. The texts incorporated into this site activation were created and collected during outreach workshops conducted at the Ukrainian Cultural Center and Ellen Mitchell Public School in the Ukrainian Village.

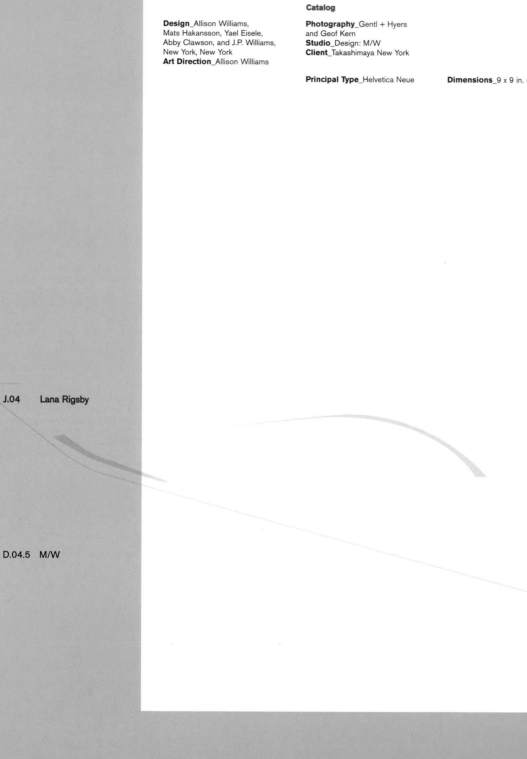

Catalog

Design_Allison Williams,
Mats Hakansson, Yael Eisele,
Abby Clawson, and J.P. Williams,
New York, New York
Art Direction_Allison Williams

Photography_Gentl + Hyers
and Geof Kern
Studio_Design: M/W
Client_Takashimaya New York

Principal Type_Helvetica Neue

Dimensions_9 x 9 in. (22.9 x 22.9 cm)

J.04   Lana Rigsby

D.04.5   M/W

 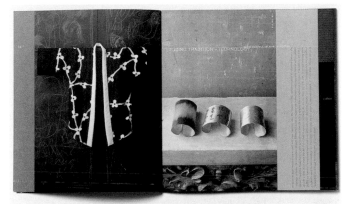

Takashimaya's most recent holiday book by Design: M/W embodies all the values that make this firm's work so deliciously special. There's no Big Idea, just lots of small ideas that are honestly conceived and lovingly, immaculately executed—that combine to create a piece that radiates purity and authenticity. At first glance, this small book is simple, clean, classic. But on closer inspection, there's a lot going on: subtle variations in typography that give emphasis to words and ideas; patterns and textures that add emotional shadings; photographic treatments that give each page a unique point of interest. All of this is managed within the sparest palette of color and typefaces. As I turned this book over and over, discovering something new each time, I kept thinking it met Albert Einstein's definition of essentiality: "things should be as simple as possible. But no simpler."

Takashimaya New York is a retail store selling unique merchandise created by artisans throughout the world. This holiday mailer, the sixth in the series created by M/W, builds upon the monochromatic palette of colors and myriad textures throughout the store. The mailer is divided into three sections: "crave" (food related), "covet" (jewelry and accessories), and "collect" (decorative home). The photography and layouts in each section reflect the subject matter; crave/food is warm and calm, covet/jewelry is eclectic, and collect/home is shot in natural surroundings in a landscape format.

D.05.5   Werner Schneider

Cards

Design_Werner Schneider,
Bad Laasphe, Germany

Calligraphy_Werner Schneider

Principal Type_Schneider-Antiqua   **Dimensions**_8¼ x 11¹¹⁄₁₆ in. (21 x 29.7 cm)

After reviewing thousands and thousands of wonderful (and some not-so-wonderful) entries, there were so many clever possibilities. I especially admired the fabulously overworked and eyeball-jarring Japanese posters, some with fluorescent velvets and rubberized flocking; I also loved the self-ironic Fifties-era packaging with their winking posterpaint silkscreen effects...but when the time came to choose one piece, this serenely classical work of exquisitely hand lettered Roman majescules sang out to me from amidst the cacophony. Werner Schneider's masterful touch is something to be treasured forever...after all, these shapes were written out directly and fluidly with wet ink filling a broad-edged dip pen, not chosen from a pre-existing drawn font. Each letter is a unique original;

each required the full attention and focus of its maker at the exact moment of its making. Schneider's piece is designed with a modern sensibility yet with an understanding of the rich history of Roman capitals from the era of classical antiquity. The quiet dignity of his presentation enhances the meaning of the text (a paean to the immutability of traditional forms); yet upon close inspection, one can detect a playfulness about the baseline and the inset characters. The power of Schneider's artwork does not depend on gimmickry, loud color, gigantic size, or attention-grabbing imagery. In the simplest of terms, blind embossing and black and white, its surpassing beauty is undeniable. Let us never forget the debt of gratitude that all typography owes its predecessor, lettering done utterly by hand.

Speaking of myself, refined forms have been my best teacher for my work as a type designer, above all Roman Capitals. Looking at the inscription on the Trajan Column awakens in me again and again a strong aesthetic feeling and fills me with a sense of deep respect. These nearly perfect forms and their qualities could not be improved upon during the 2000 years of their existence. In my reverence (admiration) for the form qualities of the Roman Caps I always try to give new

expressions to these shapes. For the understanding of form writing and drawing are the most important prerequisites. Only proficiency here guarantees a solid foundation for computerized type. For the embossed letterforms I already have design concept as a typeface. Translation of the text from the inner side: "The Roman Capitals were not intended for the day. They were to last the centuries. Their timeless beauty shines free from any patina far into the third millennium."

Brochure

Design_Jennifer Sterling and
Venus D'Amore,
San Francisco, California
Art Direction_Jennifer Sterling
Creative Direction_Jennifer
Sterling

Photography_John Casado
Design Office_Jennifer Sterling
Design
Client_Consolidated Papers

Principal Type_OCRB, Frutiger,
Futura Medium, and Not Caslon

Dimensions_9 x 12 in. (22.9 x 30.5 cm)

J.06   James Sommerville

D.06.5   Jennifer Sterling

There was some excellent work in and amongst the masses, and several pieces that interested me for different reasons. In fact, when I started to search for a single piece of work to be chosen as "my favorite" it was both interesting and fun—recycled and spat back out as difficult. To top that, I had to write a 250 word statement. I haven't written one of those since juvenile court in the early 80's. At this moment in my life, I've gone full circle in many ways and I am biased towards what I studied at school—print design. This is most likely due to the dot-com, convergent world we now live in. A world where traditional approaches to typography are being molested and "bashed out" via high powered machines that sometimes go so fast they don't remind the designer of basic fundamentals of

good type—balance, structure, composition and [the sometimes never seen these days] attention to detail. The piece I finally chose, from Jennifer Sterling, had all of those elements and more. The brochure shows genuine experimentation of typography, coupled with a classic appreciation of what good type still stands for. The text and visual timeline of each spread creates focus, leading my eye through the brochure. I knew where I was, what I should look at and in what order—which is the basis of all successful communication. From a visual point of view, the full-page photography was interesting and didn't detract from the written word, but instead created visual layers and a good hierarchy of information. Does she want a job at ATTIK?

When Consolidated Paper came to me to design their upcoming paper brochure there were few restrictions. It had to be 9 x 12" in form, and it must contain the copy provided. The copy is a wonderful narrative written on the subject of time. Originally written for the Smithsonian, it wraps the facts of time. One year (i.e. "the year of confusion") was actually 15 months long, or when the people of the time went to sleep one day only to awaken on a day that was 11 days later according to the calendar. The other restriction was that it contain absolutely no sex, drugs or religion. It was a bit difficult to discard the religion issue. After all A.D. and B.C. are not random acronyms. So I put the religion issue right up front. It is after all, how we mark time, so to discard it is more than silly it would be conceptually irresponsible. I felt the copy was wonderful yet I was hesitant to

design a historical piece. The market was designers and too many of these historical pieces just get tossed. So, how to do a futuristic piece, particularly with the issue of clothes? Who knows what would be in style in 2020? We've all done the 60's, the 70's, the 80's, and the repetition happens so quickly, I imagine soon we'll all be doing tues @ 1:30. So I dressed the models in materials that relate to paper; Saran wrap, aluminum foil, rubber matting under carpets and hired John Casado to shoot it. The purpose of using these materials was to show materials that an uncoated sheet would be unable to accurately produce on press. A photo time line runs along the bottom indicating the shots you would see if it was filmed. The type runs horizontally to depict a standard calendar format, and numerous typographic dates from the story are pulled out and used as design elements.

Work
Statement

Magazine

Design_Bill Douglas,
Toronto, Canada
Studio_The Bang

Client_Coupe

Principal Type_Trade Gothic,
Times New Roman, and Helvetica

Dimensions_9⅝ x 11½ in. (24.5 x 29.2 cm)

J.07   Anthony Vagnoni

D.07.5   Bill Douglas

Buried on the contents page of this issue of Coupe is the following observation: "We've been busy the final decade of the last thousand years huffing and puffing on the spiritual equivalent of some piece of shit stationary bicycle-slash-walking machine we purchased on a late-night infomercial while stuffing ourselves with low-fat baked Cheetos, madly pedaling, watching Springer with the headphones on while speed-reading The Celestine Prophecy." This single, ambulatory sentence summed up what I liked most about Coupe. A somewhat precious mix of art, photography, poetry, and attitude, Coupe defies conventions about the publishing business: quarterlies like this aren't supposed to exist in an age of global media consolidation. One would expect to find Coupe existing quietly as an obscure web site, yet here it is anyway, largely devoid of advertising and

defiant in its anti-commercial stance. From a design standpoint, Coupe blithely ignores current trends in its ramrod use of a single font—in this issue it's Trade Gothic, seen in a relatively limited number of variations. The effect unifies the book, and makes each editorial segment merge with the one that follows. On top of that, it's immensely readable. Content here doesn't suffer from design prerogatives that value style over clarity. Overall, I was impressed by just how clear a view of itself Coupe seems to have. That they managed to maintain this at a time when publications around the world fell all over themselves chronicling the most over-hyped event of the last hundred years—the millennium!—speaks volumes to their cocky self-assurance.

Coupe is both a commentary on, and a reaction to the information age we live in. Featured on the cover of Coupe 2 is a 220 word text block set a la legal fine print describing in detail what awaits the reader on the inside. "Yes, we've added great new departments such as our sassy *"Who's Hot, Who's Not,"* where we tell you who's hot and who's not; and you'll love our new section called *"What's Hot, What's Not"*, where we tell you what's hot and what's not...In this issue we take

an in-depth look at America's newest sweetheart, Britney Spears (pg. 147)". There is no Britney Spears interview. There isn't even a page 147. Instead, featured is the work of artists, photographers, and writers, printed using five colours on two different paper stocks and weights, melted down and melded together to create a singular work in which the past and future collide head-on.

Typography 21
The Annual of Typography

2|21

TypeDirectorsClub
Selected Entries

TDC 46+ P.035

Design_Joe Scorsone
and Alice Drueding
Jenkintown, Pennsylvania
Art Direction_Joe Scorsone

Design Office_Scorsone/Drueding

Principal Type_Monoline Script,
Schwere, and Franklin Gothic Extra
Condensed

Dimensions_30 ⁷⁄₁₆ x 22 ⁷⁄₁₆ in. (78 x 58 cm)

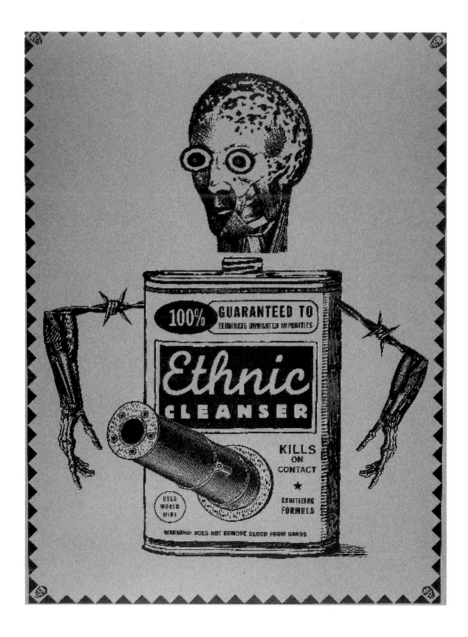

Design_Jason Schulte
Minneapolis, Minnesota
Art Direction_Charles S. Anderson
Copywriter_Lisa Pemrick

Design Office_Charles S.
Anderson Design
Client_French Paper Company

Principal Type_Alpin Gothic
and ITC Franklin Gothic

Dimensions_35 x 48 in.
(88.9 x 121.9 cm)

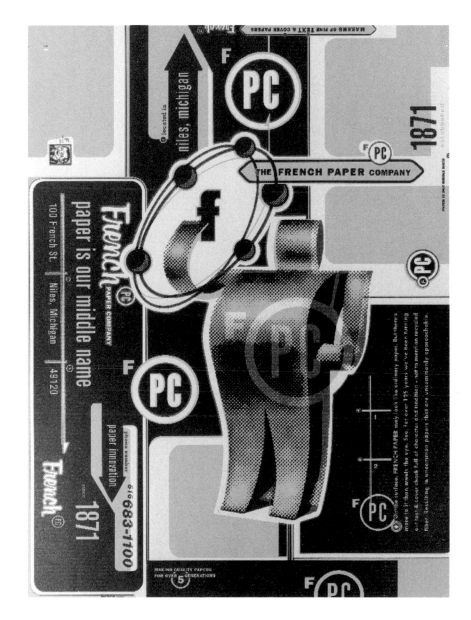

Design_Laurie DeMartino
Minneapolis, Minnesota
Art Direction_Laurie DeMartino
Printer_Rodgers Litho

Studio_Studio d Design
Client_Tulsa Art Directors Club

Principal Type_Franklin Gothic
(metal), News Gothic BT, ITC New
Baskerville, and handlettering

Dimensions_24 x 31⅝ in. (61 x 80.3 cm)

Design_Uwe Melichar and
Katrin Schmidt
Hamburg, Germany
Art Direction_Uwe Melichar
Creative Direction_Uwe Melichar

Design Office_Factor Design
Client_HKF Film–und
Fernsehproduktion

Principal Type_Bank Gothic,
Alternate Gothic, and Ariston BQ

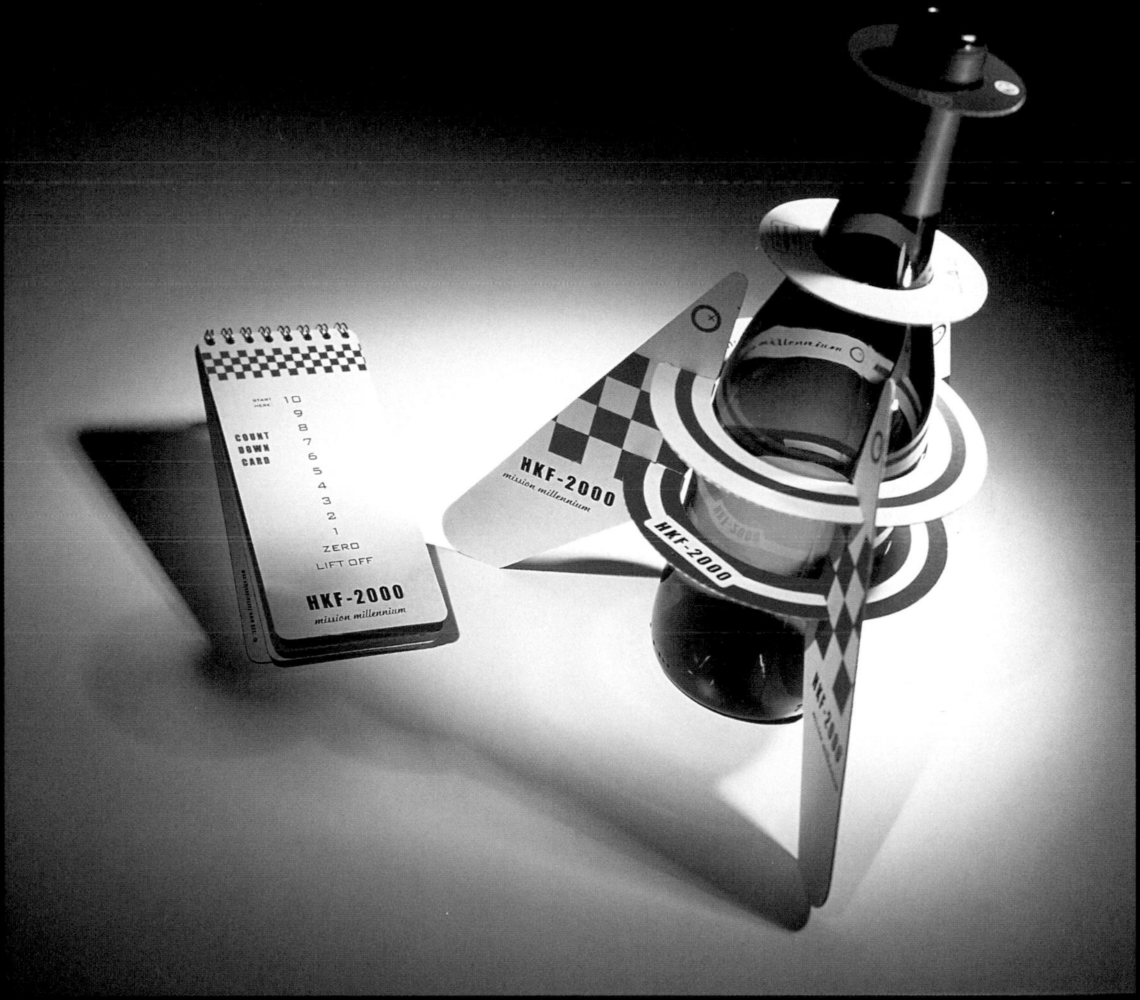

Poster

Design_Takafumi Kusagaya
and Miki Sekigushi
Tokyo, Japan
Art Direction_Takafumi Kusagaya

Design Office_Kusagaya Design, Inc.
Client_Takeo, Inc.

Principal Type_Original type
Takafumi Miyajima

Dimensions_28⁷⁄₁₆ x 40 ⁹⁄₁₆ in.
(72.8 x 103 cm)

Poster

Design_Paul Bichler
Chicago, Illinois
Art Direction_Paul Bichler
Creative Direction_Chris Froeter

Design Office_Froeter Design Co., Inc.
Client_The David and Alfred Smart
Museum of Art

Principal Type_OCR-B and
DIN Mittelschrift

Dimensions_24 x 18 in. (61 x 45.7 cm)

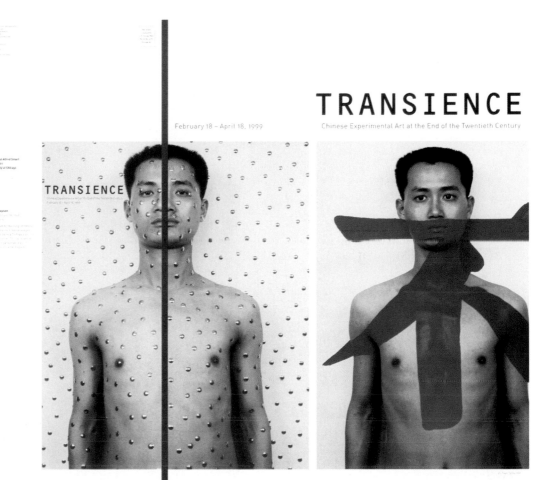

Poster

Design_Fons M. Hickmann
Berlin, Germany
Lettering_Tom Croll's Mother
Art Direction_Fons M. Hickmann

Creative Direction_Fons M.
Hickmann
Studio_Fons M. Hickmann
Client_Theaterhau

Principal Type_Tom Croll's
Mother's Typewriter

Dimensions_39⅜ x 27⁹⁄₁₆ in.
(100 x 70 cm)

Invitation

Design_David Salanitro
and Ted Bluey,
San Francisco, California
Art Direction_David Salanitro
Creative Direction_David Salanitro
Illustration_Heather Layne

Design Office_Oh Boy,
A Design Company
Client_Tracy Chaney

Principal Type_Century Schoolbook
and Twentieth Century

Dimensions_4 ⅞ x 6 ⅞ in.
(12.4 x 17.4 cm)

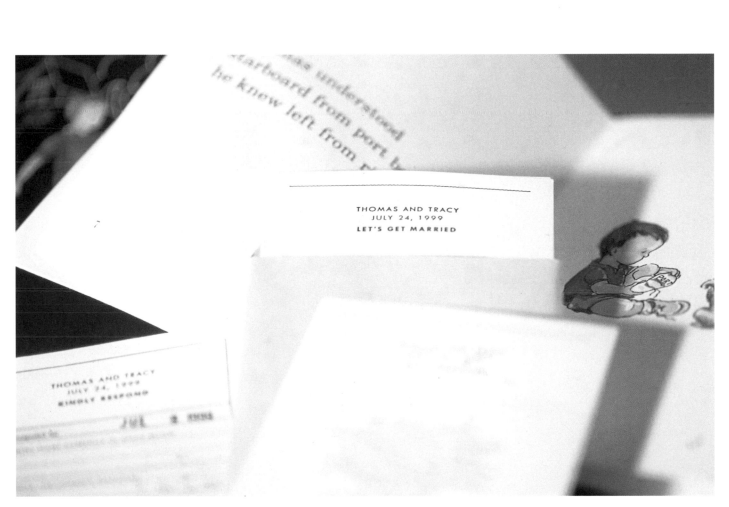

Poster

Design_Laurie DeMartino
Minneapolis, Minnesota
Art Direction_Laurie DeMartino
Photography_Aaron Dimmel
Seed Art Illustration_David
Steinlicht
Printer_Holm Graphic Service

Studio_Studio d Design
Client_Art Directors Association
of Iowa

Principal Type_Handlettering
with seeds

Dimensions_17 x 24 in.
(43.2 x 61 cm)

Design_Akihiko Tsukamoto
Tokyo, Japan
Art Direction_Akihiko Tsukamoto
Printer_Twin-Eight Co., Ltd.

Studio_Zuan Club
Client_Amaguri-Taro, Inc.

Principal Type_ITC Snap Italic,
ITC Kokoa, and Hiragino Gyosho
Extra Bold

Dimensions_40 ⁵⁄₁₆ x 28 ⁵⁄₁₆ in.
(103 x 72.8 cm)

Design_Heribert Birnbach
Bonn, Germany
Art Direction_Heribert Birnbach
Creative Direction_Heribert
Birnbach
Printer_Warlich Druck,
Meckenheim

Design Office_Birnbach Design
Client_Fringe Ensemble Frank
Heuel Theater im Ballsaal

Principal Type_FF Scratch
and FF Thesis

Dimensions_23 ⅜ x 33 ⅛ in.
(59.84 x 84.1 cm)

Wenedikt Jerofejew

Die Reise nach Petuschki
Ein Poem/Ein Theaterstück

Eine Produktion des
fringe ensemble Frank Heuel
in Coproduktion mit dem
Forum Freies Theater, Düsseldorf

Design_Laurie DeMartino
Minneapolis, Minnesota
Art Direction_Laurie DeMartino
Photography_Laurie DeMartino
Printer_Williamson Printing
Corporation
Paper_French Paper Company

Studio_Studio d Design
Client_American Institute of
Graphic Design/Minnesota

Principal Type_News Gothic
and ITC New Baskerville

Dimensions_Various

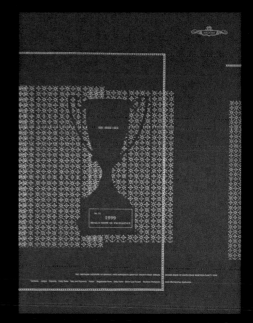

Design_Catherine Knaeble
Minneapolis, Minnesota
Lettering_Elvis Swift
Art Direction_Catherine Knaeble
Creative Direction_Connie
Soteropolis

Design Office_Dayton's/Hudson's/
Marshall Field's

Principal Type_Bembo, Harting,
and handlettering

Dimensions_Various

Poster and Brochure

Design_Veress Tamás
Budapest, Hungary
Lettering_Veress Tamás
Art Direction_Veress Tamás
Creative Direction_Simon Attila
Illustration_Veress Tamás

Studio_Art Force Studio

Principal Type_Gill Sans
and handlettering

Dimensions_16 9/16 x 23 1/4 in.
(42 x 59 cm)

Design_Scott Ray
Dallas, Texas
Lettering_Scott Ray
Art Direction_Scott Ray
Creative Direction_Scott Ray
Photography_Doug Davis
Copywriter_Dorit Suffness

Design Office_Peterson & Company
Client_Dallas Society of Visual
Communications

Principal Type_Handlettered

Dimensions_22 x 32 ¼
(55.9 x 81.9 cm)

Design_Matteo Federico Bologna
New York, New York
Art Direction_Matteo
Federico Bologna
Illustration_Robert Padilla

Studio_Mucca Design Corporation
Client_Pastis Restaurant

Principal Type_Pastis Nobel,
Pastis Rockwell, and Pastis
Geometric Slab Condensed
Tamaye Parry

Dimensions_Various

PASTIS

CAFÉ, LIQUEURS & BIÈRES DE MARQUE

CUISINE TRADITIONNELLE RECOMMANDÉE

CAFE – COMPTOIR – RESTAURANT

COCKTAILS AU PASTIS
- 8.00 -

LE CASSE-TÊTE
Anejo Rum, Cognac, Calvados, Pernod

LE CHRYSANTHÈME
Benedictine, Dry Vermouth, Suze

LE FEU ROUGE
Stoli Pepper Vodka, Ricard, Fresh Lemon Juice

LE SAZERAC
Bourbon, Fresh Lemon Juice, Cesanis

LE PERROQUET
Pernod and Mint Syrup

L'AMANDE PASTIS
Ricard, Almond Syrup and Soda Water

Coffee	2.00
Espresso	2.50
Cappuccino	3.00
Café au Lait	3.00

HORS D'OEUVRES

Onion Soup Gratinée	6.00
Leeks Vinaigrette	7.00
Beet, Endive, Roquefort and Walnut Salad	8.00
Rillettes Fermière	8.00
Mixed Green Salad ....7.00 w/Goat Cheese	8.00
Grilled Sardines	8.00
Pissaladière - Caramelized Onion Tart	6.00
Frisée Lardons and a Poached Egg	8.00
Gratin of Mussels and Spinach	7.00
Grilled Octopus and White Bean Salad	9.00
Oysters on the Half Shell	P/A
Fritto Misto	11.00

ENTREES

Skate au Beurre Noir	15.00
Grilled Salmon, Sauce Verte	16.00
Trout Amandine	16.00
Shellfish Stew w/Chorizo	15.00
Grilled Whole Fish of the Day	P/A
Half Roast Lobster w/Garlic Butter and Fries	P/A
Full Roast Lobster w/Garlic Butter and Fries	P/A
Poussin Rôti with Garlic Confit	16.00
Glazed Pork w/Lentils	17.00
Roast Leg of Lamb w/Flageolets	16.00
Steak Frites w/Béarnaise	17.00
Butcher's Tender w/Marrow and Shallots	18.00
Blanquette de Veau	16.00
Tripes Gratinées	14.00
Braised Beef w/Glazed Carrots	17.00

PATES

Penne Puttanesca	13.00
Spaghetti Carbonara	12.00
Mushroom Ravioli w/Sage and Butter	12.00
Rabbit Pappardelle	14.00
Penne Primavera	13.00

GARNITURES

Légumes Verts	4.50
Ratatouille	5.00
Carottes Vichy	4.50
French Fries	5.00
Gratin Dauphinois	5.50

– CARAFE MAISON –

BLANC

CÔTES DE GASCOGNE
verre 6.00 / demi 10.00 / carafe 13.00

BORDEAUX BLANC
verre 7.00 / demi 11.00 / carafe 15.00

ROUGE

VINS DE PAYS D'OC '94
verre 6.00 / demi 10.00 / carafe 14.00

MARCILLAC '97
verre 7.00 / demi 11.00 / carafe 15.00

BREAKFAST	TOUTE LA SEMAINE	8.00 AM - 12.00 PM
LUNCH	MONDAY FRIDAY	12.00 PM - 5.00 PM
DINNER	TOUTE LA SEMAINE	6.00 PM - 12.00 AM
SUPPER	SUNDAY THURSDAY	12.00 AM - 2.00 AM
	FRIDAY SATURDAY	12.00 AM - 3.00 AM
BRUNCH	SATURDAY SUNDAY	12.00 PM - 4.00 PM

20% gratuities added to parties of 8 or more

CHEFS DE CUISINE
Riad Nasr & Lee Hanson

DINNER

TARIF DES CONSOMMATIONS

HORS D'OEUVRES

	TAXES AND SERVICE NOT INCLUDED
Onion Soup Gratinée	6.00
Leeks Vinaigrette	7.00
Beet, Endive and Walnut Salad	8.00
Rillettes Fermière	8.00
Mixed Green Salad	6.00
Mixed Green Salad with Goat Cheese	7.00
Grilled Sardines	8.00
Pissaladière - Caramelized Onion Tart	6.00
Frisée Lardons with a Poached Egg	8.00
Gratin of Mussels and Spinach	7.00
Grilled Octopus and White Bean Salad	9.00
Oysters on the Half Shell	P/A
Fritto Misto	11.00

SALADES

Grilled Chicken Paillard	14.00
Salade Niçoise	14.00
Grilled Vegetable Salad	12.00

SANDWICHS

Pressed Mozzarella, Basil and Peperonata	9.00
Confit of Pork and Chutney	10.00
Hamburger	9.00
Cheeseburger	8.00
Hamburger à Cheval	10.00
Omelette aux Fines Herbes w/French Fries	10.00

PATES

	TAXES AND SERVICE NOT INCLUDED
Penne Puttanesca	13.00
Spaghetti Carbonara	12.00
Mushroom Ravioli with Sage and Butter	12.00
Rabbit Pappardelle	14.00
Penne Primavera	13.00

ENTREES

Skate au Beurre Noir	
Grilled Salmon, Sauce Verte	
Trout Amandine	
Shellfish Stew with Chorizo	
Grilled Whole Fish of the Day	
Half or Full Roast Lobster with French Fries	
Poussin Rôti with Garlic Confit	
Glazed Pork with Lentils	
Roast Leg of Lamb with Flageolets	
Steak Frites with Béarnaise	
Butcher's Tender with Marrow and Shallots	
Blanquette de Veau	
Tripes Gratinées	
Braised Beef with Glazed Carrots	

GARNITURES

Légumes Verts	
Ratatouille	
Carottes Vichy	
French Fries	
Gratin Dauphinois	

20% gratuities added to parties of 10 or more

CHEFS DE CUISINE Riad Nasr & Lee Hanson

PASTIS

DESSERTS $6

Apple Tart
Crêpes Suzette
Ile Flottante
Riz au Lait (Rice Pudding)
Gratin de Fruits
Tarte Tropézienne
Mousse au Chocolat
Poire Belle-Hélène,
(Poached Pear with Vanilla Ice Cream & Chocolate Sauce)
Tarte au Citron
Pastis Chocolate Layer Cake

Ice Cream/Sorbet $5

DESSERT WINES

Muscat de Rivesaltes Gautier '97		Beaumes de Venise Beaumetric '96	
Glass	6.00	Glass	8.00
Half Bottle	15.00	Half Bottle	18.00

PASTIS

CAFE · COMPTOIR · RESTAURANT

9 Ninth Avenue – New York · NY 10014
Phone (212) 929.4844 · Fax (212) 929.5676
E-mail: frontdesk@pastisny.com

PASTIS

BISTROT FRANÇAIS

Little West 12th Street
(corner of ninth avenue)
☎ (212) 929 4844

CUISINE TRADITIONNELLE

PASTIS

BUVEZ UN **PASTIS** APÉRITIF ANISÉ

Design_Thomas Leifer
and Sandra Schlichting
Hamburg, Germany
Art Direction_Thomas Leifer

Design Office_Factor Design
Client_Henkels Gestaltet

Principal Type_OCR-B

Dimensions_11 ⁹⁄₁₆ x 6 ¾ in.
(29.4 x 17.2 cm)

Design_Frank Sarfati, Oliver Sténuit, and Joël Van Audenhaege
Brussels, Belgium
Art Direction_Frank Sarfati, Oliver Sténuit, and
Joël Van Audenhaege

Agency_[sign*]
Client_Milly Films

Principal Type_Copperplate Gothic   **Dimensions**_Vari

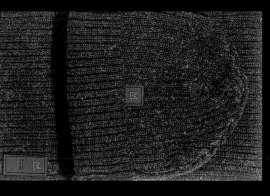

Design_ Jennifer Sterling
San Francisco, California
Art Direction_ Jennifer Sterling
Creative Direction_ Jennifer Sterling

Design Office_ Jennifer Sterling
Design
Client_ Spike Networks

Principal Type_ Garamond No. 3,
Orator, and Cottonwood

Dimensions_ Various

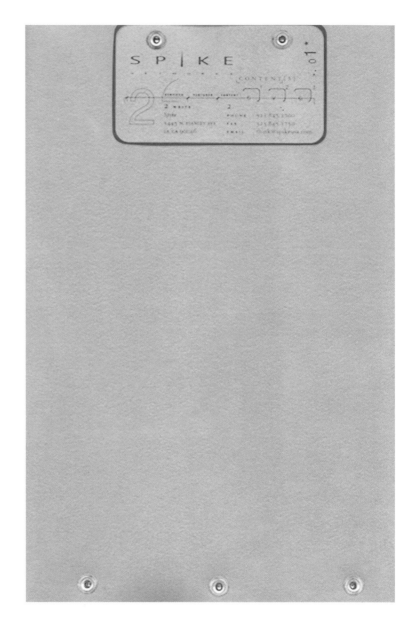

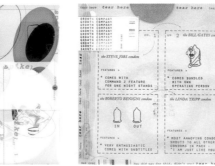

Design_David Covell and Joe Peila
Burlington, Vermont
Art Direction_David Covell
Creative Direction_Michael Jager

Studio_Jager Di Paola Kemp Design
Client_Champion International

Principal Type_Nobel, Trade Gothic,
and Russell Square

Dimensions_37 ¼ x 22 ½ in.
(94.6 x 57.2 cm)

Catalog

Design_Anuthin Wongsunkakon
Bangkok, Thailand
Art Direction_Anuthin Wongsunkakon

Studio_Graphic Behaviour
Client_Type Behaviour and
Kitsch Publishing

Principal Type_Son Gothic,
Key Stone State, Aspirin,
and Metamorphosis

Dimensions_4 x 6 in. (10.2 x 15.2 cm)
and 4 x 8 in. (10.2 x 20. 3 cm)

Design_Michael Petersen
Chicago, Illinois
Lettering_Mchael Petersen
Art Direction_Ken Fox and
Michael Petersen

Agency_VSA Partners
Client_Harley-Davidson
Motor Company

Principal Type_Akzidenz Grotesk,
Bulmer, Trade Gothic, and
handlettering

Dimensions_24 x 36 in.
(61 x 91.4 cm)

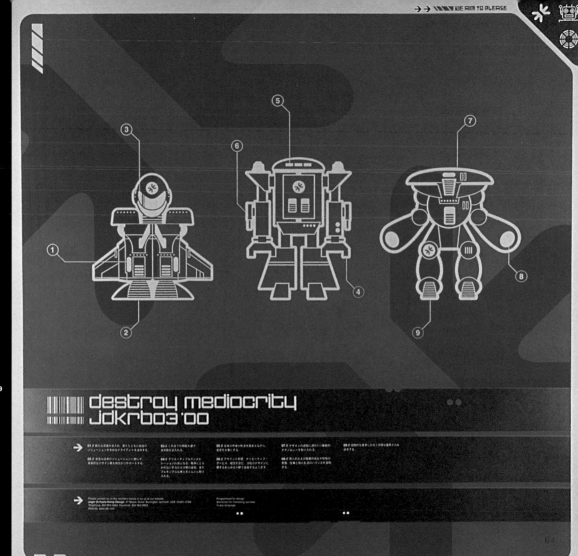

destroy mediocrity
jdkrbo3 '00

Design_Leslie Chan Wing Kei
Taipei, Taiwan
Lettering_Leslie Chan Wing Kei
Art Direction_Leslie Chan Wing Kei
Creative Direction_Leslie Chan
Wing Kei
Photography_Justin Chin
and Larcher Chao

Design Office_Leslie Chan
Design Co., Ltd.
Client_Macau Designers
Association

Principal Type_Chapbook

Dimensions_39 ⅜ x 27 ⁹⁄₁₆ in.
(100 x 70 cm)

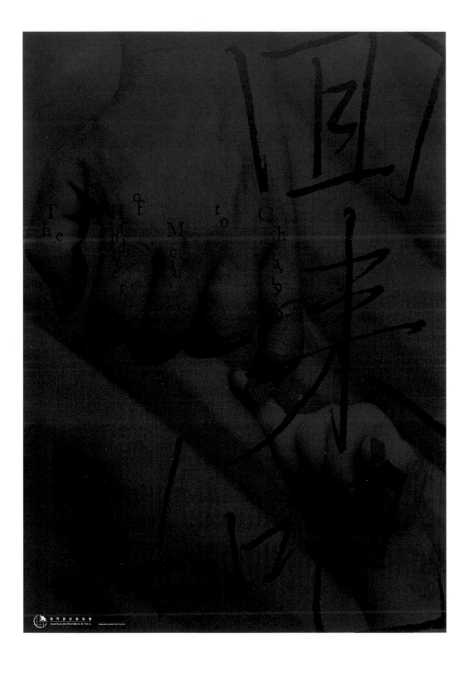

Campaign

Design_Lance Rusoff and
Jeremy Dean
Philadelphia, Pennsylvania
Art Direction_Lance Rusoff
and Jeremy Dean
Creative Direction_Sue Otto

Studio_Urban Outfitters

Principal Type_Helvetica

Dimensions_18 x 36 in.
(45.7 x 91.4 cm)

Campaign

Design_Todd Piper-Hauswirth,
Charles S. Anderson,
Jason Schulte, Kyle Hames,
and P.J. Chmiel
Minneapolis, Minnesota
Art Direction_Charles S. Anderson
Illustration_Charles S. Anderson
and Kyle Hames
Copywriter_Lisa Pemrick

Design Office_Charles S.
Anderson Design
Client French Paper Company

Principal Type_Trade Gothic
and Univers

Dimensions_Various

Brochure

Design_Tom Brown
Coquitlam, British Columbia, Canada
Art Direction_Tom Brown

Studio_TBA+D
Client_Fredrik Broden

Principal Type_Akzidenz Grotesk

Dimensions_3 ⅝ x 5 in.
(9.2 x 12.7 cm)

Brochure

Design_Michael Bierut
and Jacqueline Thaw
New York, New York
Art Direction_Michael Bierut
Photography_Melissa Hayden,
Neal Slavin, Maria Robledo,
Emily Mott, Byron Lee, and
Shepard Fairey
Illustration_Andy Cruz, Rich Roat,
and Christoph Niemann

Editors_Michael Bierut
and Jacqueline Thaw
Writers_Michael Bierut,
Andrea Moed, Lorraine Wild,
Peter Hall, Andrew Tilin,
Steven Heller, and Stuart Henley
Design Office_Pentagram
Client_Mohawk Paper Mills

Principal Type_Vendetta, Cooper
Black, and Alternate Gothic

Dimensions_7 x 4 ¼ in.
(17.8 x 10.8 cm)

Chuck Barnard: Driving down Fremont Street in the early 1960s was an experience like visiting the Grand Canyon. There was exotic lighting going off in every direction on all sides, you could even hear the things, clicking and buzzing. Entire buildings were wrapped in neon. It was like a drive-in sign. You'd drive around the block and come back and go through it again. That was the way it was when neon was king.

Poster

Design_Shuichi Nogami
Osaka, Japan
Art Direction_Shuichi Nogami

Design Office_Nogami Design Office

Principal Type_Tear Drop

Dimensions_40 ⁹⁄₁₆ x 28 ⁷⁄₁₆ in.
(103 x 72.8 cm)

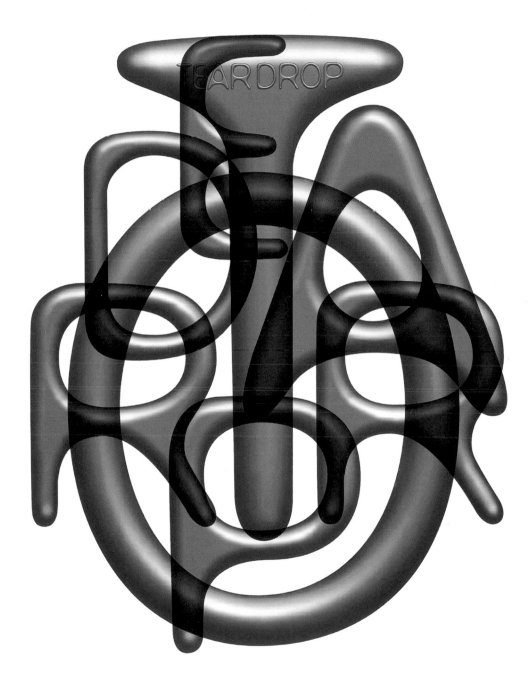

Design_Jennifer Sterling
San Francisco, California
Lettering_Jennifer Sterling
Creative Direction_Jennifer Sterling
Art Direction_Jennifer Sterling
Creative Direction_Jennifer Sterling

Design Office_Jennifer Sterling
Design

Principal Type_Garamond No. 3,
FF Meta, and handlettering

Dimensions_6 x 9 in.
(15.2 x 22.9 cm)

Design_Paula Scher
and Keith Daigle
New York, New York
Art Direction_Paula Scher

Design Office_Pentagram
Client_Metropolis

Principal Type_Helvetica

Dimensions_24 x 18 in.
(61 x 45.7 cm)

Design_Slavimir Stojanovic
Ljubljana, Slovenia
Art Direction_Slavimir Stojanovic
Creative Direction_Slavimir
Stojanovic

Design Studio_Kompas Design
Client_JDP

Principal Type_Helvetica Black

Dimensions_26 x 18 ⅛ in.
(66 x 46 cm)

Design_Scott Lambert
Los Angeles, California
Art Direction_Scott Lambert
Creative Direction_Douglas Joseph
Photography_Eric Tucker
Writer_Scott Lambert

Design Office_Douglas Joseph
Partners
Client_Spicers Paper Inc.

Principal Type_Perpetua,
Bell Gothic, Variex, and Univers

Dimensions_7 x 8 ½ in.
(17.8 x 21.6 cm)

Our Mega-tek team (left to right): Glenn Freakley PhD., Senior Researcher. Glenn heads the laser proton voice activated system division. Alfred Borngold, Product Engineer. Alfred has guided the Interface cranial consol development team since 1999. Wil DeSord, Senior Vice President of Product Development. Wil joined the Interface team in late 1998 and has worked extensively on the communications device system which drives the laser network.

Research & Development   The Rap'd Communication Matrix (RCM) market is rapidly growing and the Etek R&D group is moving to capitalize from sales of the Interface product. To meet the market demands, Eteknologies is developing new light-speed laser algorithms, engineering new light-weight helmet materials and creating focused solutions that will enable our customers to embrace the latest teknology.
Eteknologies R&D investment, which remained strong at 32% of revenues in fiscal 2005, will continue to be a key component of our company strategy.

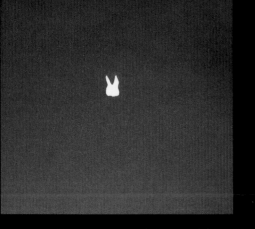

BESONDERE Präzision erfordert die sogenannte Kombinationstechnik, bei der fester und herausnehmbarer Zahnersatz über spezielle Verankerungselemente verbunden sind. Hierzu dienen zum Beispiel Geschiebe, Druckknopfverankerungen, Stege oder Doppelkronen.

ZAHNERSATZ dieser Art ist im Behandlungsablauf und in der zahntechnischen Herstellung sehr aufwendig. Er ist hinsichtlich Ästhetik und

Abb. 13

Claude Mouton (gest. 1786) erfand eine Prothesenbasis mit kleinen, den Zahnfächern ähnelnden Löchern, in denen nach oben Stifte herausragten, auf die echte menschliche Zähne aufgesetzt wurden, die knapp unterhalb des Zahnhalses abgeschnitten worden waren.

Sicherheit vielfach den klammerverankerten Prothesen überlegen

DIESE VORTEILE kommen jedoch nur zum Tragen, wenn die einzelnen Elemente mit äußerster Genauigkeit aufeinander abgestimmt sind und sich zu einem funktionstüchtigen und harmonischen Ganzen verbinden. In Zusammenarbeit mit den Zahnärzten kreative Lösungen zu entwickeln und minutiös zu realisieren gehört zu den Ansprüchen, die wir an uns selbst stellen.

Abb. 13) Der Franzose Pierre Fauchard (1678 bis 1761) fasste das zahnmedizinische Wissen der westlichen Welt zu seiner Zeit zusammen und optimatisierte es. In seinem Werk «Le chirurgien dentiste» (1728) gibt er einen Überblick über die damalige Brücken- und Prothesentechnik.

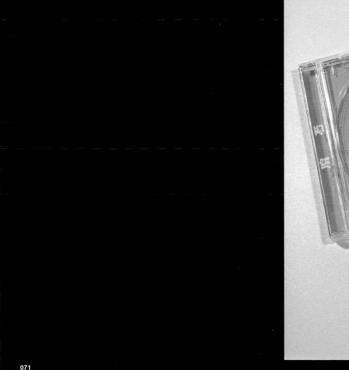

Brochure

Design_Susanne Fritsch,
Andreas Uebele, and
Jutta Boxheimer
Stuttgart, Germany
Lettering_Jutta Boxheimer
Art Direction_Andreas Uebele
and Susanne Fritsch

Agency_Büro Uebele,
Visuelle Kommunikation
Client_Lothar Bertrams

Principal Type_Akzidenz Grotesk

Dimensions_8 ¾ x 11 ⅞ in.
(22.3 x 30.2 cm)

Design_Mark Geer
Houston, Texas
Creative Direction_Mark Geer

Studio_Geer Design Inc.
Client_Domtar Paper

Principal Type_Caslon Oldstyle
No.337, Rosewood Fill, Linotext,
and Texas Hero

Dimensions_8 ⅜ x 11 ¾ in.
(21.3 x 29.9 cm)

Every educated man during the Middle Ages and Renaissance knew his sign and planet. The Church sponsored several schools of astronomy which incorporated astrology. Astromica, the study of astronomy, supplied the base knowledge; while astrologia, the study of astrology, was its applied science

Habit d' Astrologue.

Costume for an Astrologer
PUBLISHED BY GERARD VALCK c.1690 (ENGRAVING). GERMAN SCHOOL, 17TH CENTURY

Design_Michael Daiminger
Munich, Germany
Creative Direction_Michael
Daiminger and Claus Lehmann
Photography_Infrarot GmbH

Design Office_Infrarot GmbH
Client_Fastfood Theater

Principal Type_Berthold Akzidenz
Grotesk Condensed

Dimensions_23 ⅜ x 33 ⅛ in.
(53.4 x 84.1 cm)

Design_Shuichi Nogami
Osaka, Japan
Art Direction_Shuichi Nogami

Design Office_Nogami
Design Office
Client_Japan Typography Association

Principal Type_Tear Drop

Dimensions_23 ⅜ x 33 ⅛ in.
(59.4 x 84.1 cm)

It's new typeface originally designed by N.D.O.

Brochure

Design_Jon Olsen
Portland, Oregon
Art Direction_Jon Olsen

Creative Direction_Steve Sandstrom
Illustration_Jeff Foster
and John Hersey
Copywriter_Matt Elhardt

Principal Type_Century Schoolbook

Dimensions_8 ½ x 11 in.
(21.6 x 27.9 cm)

Brochure

Design_Venus D'Amore
and Erik Olsen
San Francisco, California
Art Direction_Erik Olsen

Design Office_Erik Olsen
Graphic Design
Client_Spinal Diagnostics
and Treatment Center

Principal Type_Avenir

Dimensions_5 x 8 in.
(12.7 x 20.3 cm)

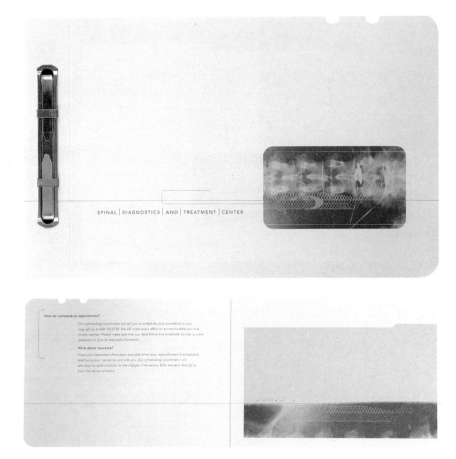

Design_David Handschuh
Urbana, Illinois
School_University of Illinois
Urbana-Champaign

Client_Montage

Principal Type_Typewriter, Times
New Roman, and handlettering

Dimensions_6 ¼ x 7 ⅛ in.
(15.9 x 18.1 cm)

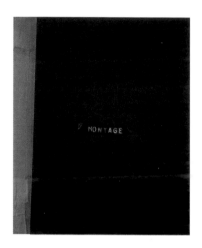

Brochure

Design_Giorgio Pesce
Lausanne, Switzerland
Art Direction_Giorgio Pesce
Creative Direction_Giorgio Pesce

Agency_Atelier Poisson
Client_Théâtre Arsenic

Principal Type_Triumvirate
and Trade Gothic

Dimensions_Envelope:
7 5/16 x 3 3/8 in. (19.5 x 8 cm)
Program: 21 5/16 x 5/16 in.
(54.2 x 2.1 cm)

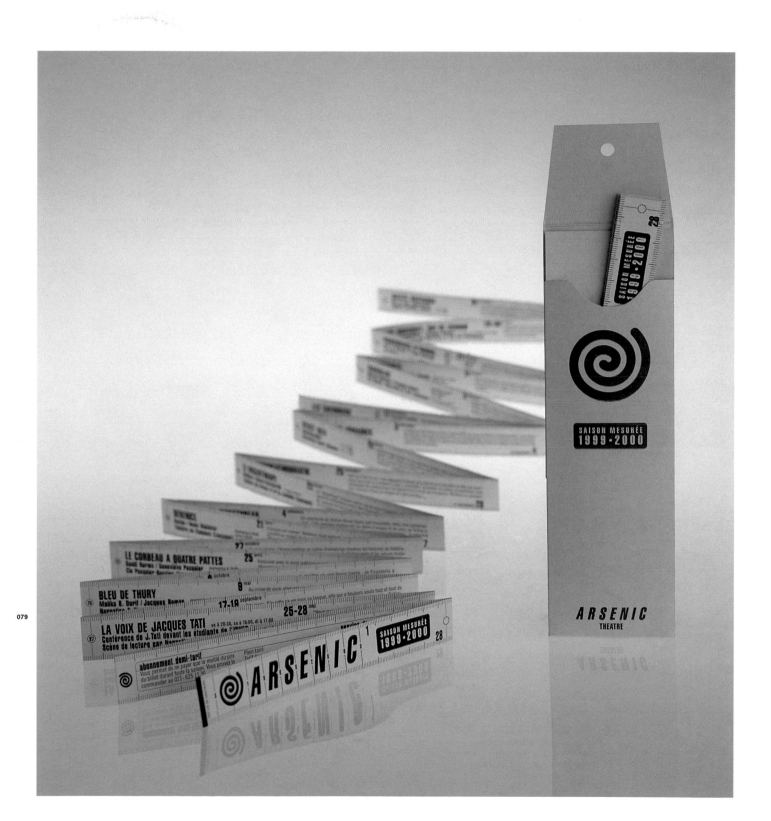

Design_Aaron Dietz
Farmington, Connnecticut
Art Direction_Aaron Dietz
Creative Direction_Mike Scricco
Illustration_James Yang,
Laura Ljungkvist, and Jack Unruh

Agency_Keiler & Company
Client_Crane's

Principal Type_Jigsaw,
Subluxation, and Mrs. Eaves

Dimensions_6 x 9 in.
(15.2 x 22.5 cm)

Farmington, Connnecticut
Lettering_Carolyn Fisher
Art Direction_Liz Dzilenski
Creative Direction_Mike Scricco
Illustration_Ed Fotheringham,
Nishan Akgulian, Eric Panke,
Raymond Verdaguet, and
Carolyn Fisher

Client_Crane's

Principal Type_Mrs. Eaves,
Isonorm, and handlettering

Dimensions_6 x 9 in.
(15.2 x 22.5 cm)

Poster

Design_Frank Baseman
Jenkintown, Pennsylvania
Art Direction_Frank Baseman
Creative Direction_Frank Baseman
Photography_Frank Baseman

Studio_Frank Baseman Design
Client_Philadelphia College of
Textiles & Science

Principal Type_Bulmer, Egiziano,
Kuenstler Script, and ITC Franklin
Gothic Extra Condensed

Dimensions_19 ½ x 26 in.
(49.5 x 66 cm)

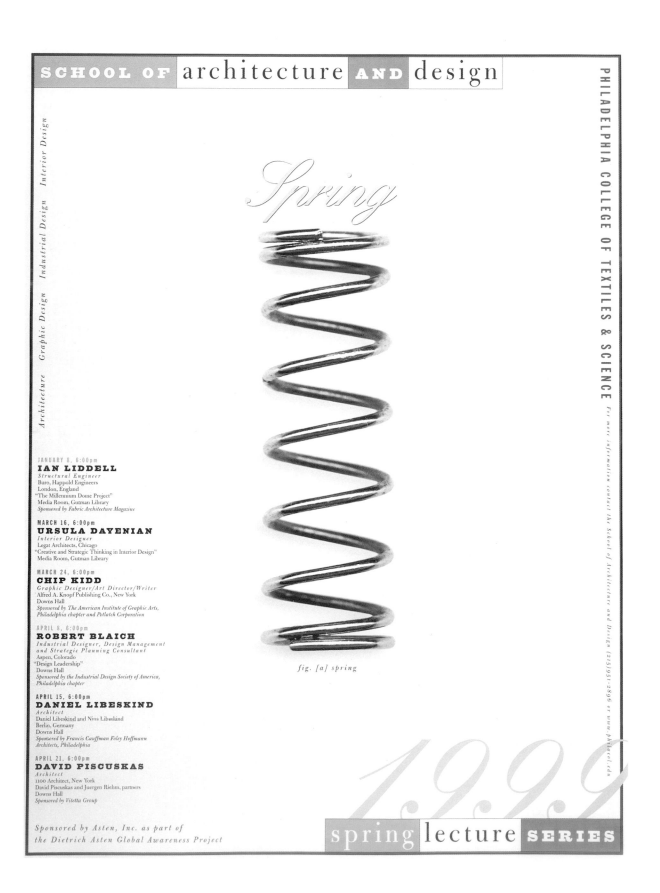

fig. [a] spring

Brochure

Design_Clive Piercy
Santa Monica, California
Art Direction_Clive Piercy
and Michael Hodgson

Design Office_Ph.D
Client_Friend + Johnson

Principal Type_Trade Gothic,
Perpetua, and Interstate

Dimensions_7 x 11 in.
(17.8 x 27.9 cm)

Catalog

Design_Vanessa Eckstein
and Frances Chen
Toronto, Canada
Art Direction_Vanessa Eckstein

Design Studio_Blok Design
Client_The Partners Film Company

Principal Type_Trade Gothic

Dimensions_8 ½ x 11 in.
(21.6 X 27.9 cm)

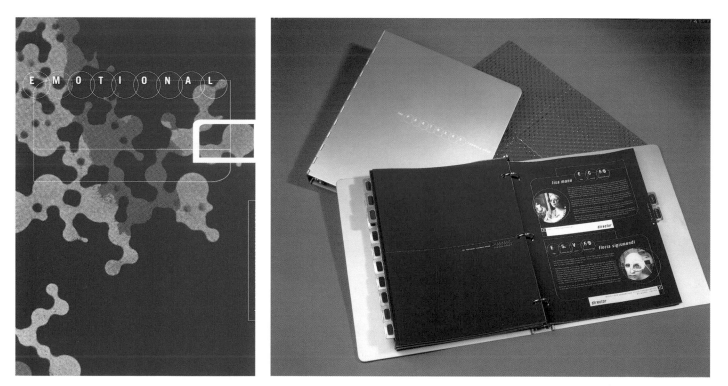

Poster

Design_Lanny Sommese
State College, Pennsylvania
Art Direction_Lanny Sommese
Creative Direction_Lanny Sommese

Studio_Sommese Design
Client_Penn State School
of Visual Arts

Principal Type_Gill Sans
and Helvetica

Dimensions_26 x 40 in.
(66 x 101.6 cm)

Poster

Design_Catherine Knaeble
and Karl Wolf
Minneapolis, Minnesota
Lettering_Elvis Swift
Art Direction_Catherine Knaeble
Creative Direction_Connie
Soteropolis

Design Office_Dayton's/Hudson's/
Marshall Field's

Principal Type_Bembo, Harting,
and handlettering

Dimensions_22 x 28 in.
(55.9 x 71.1 cm) and
14 x 22 in. (35.6 x 55.9 cm)

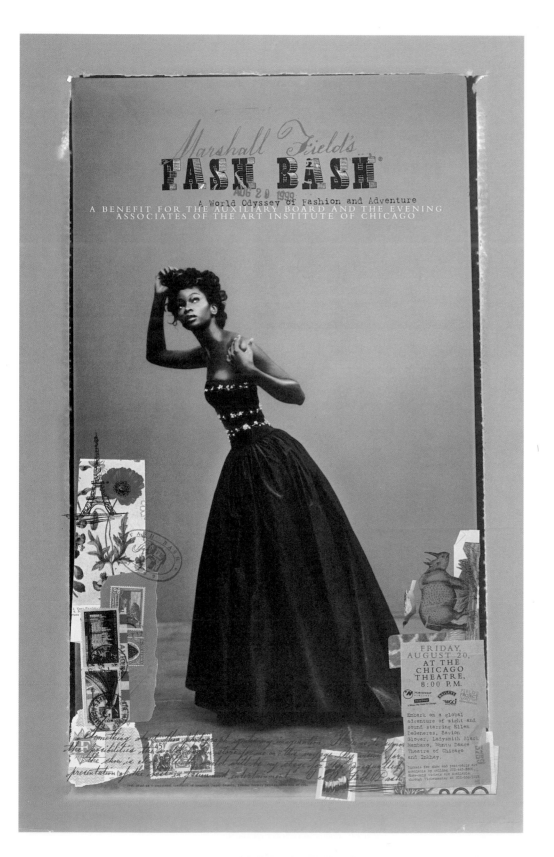

Design_Steve Sandstrom
Portland, Oregon
Art Direction_Steve Sandstrom
Creative Direction_Steve Sandstrom

Principal Type_Aviator

Dimensions_10 ½ x 5 x 3 in.
(26.7 x 12.7 x 7.6 cm)

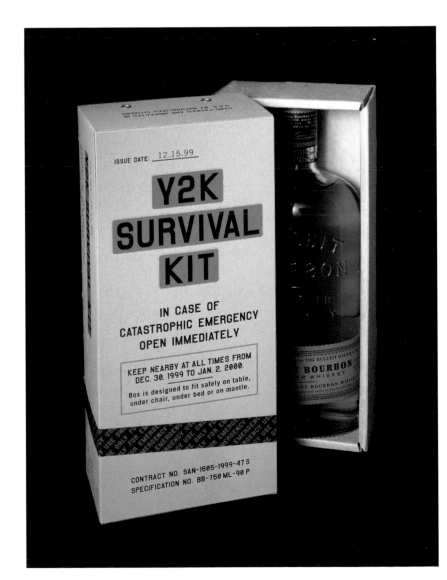

Design_Shinnoske Sugisaki
Osaka, Japan
Art Direction_Shinnoske Sugisaki
Creative Direction_Nob Fukuda
Copywriter_Osamu Nakasuji

Studio_Shinnoske Inc.
Client_Tojuso Center

Principal Type_Morisawa MB31
and Morisawa MB101

Dimensions_21 ¼ x 15 ¾ in.
(54 x 40 cm)

Poster

Design_Pedro Falcão
Lisbon, Portugal
Art Direction_Pedro Falcão
Photography_Mariana Viegas

Studio_Secretonix
Client_André Guedes

Principal Type_ITC Charter

Dimensions_16 ⅝ x 23 ⅝ in.
(42 x 60.5 cm)

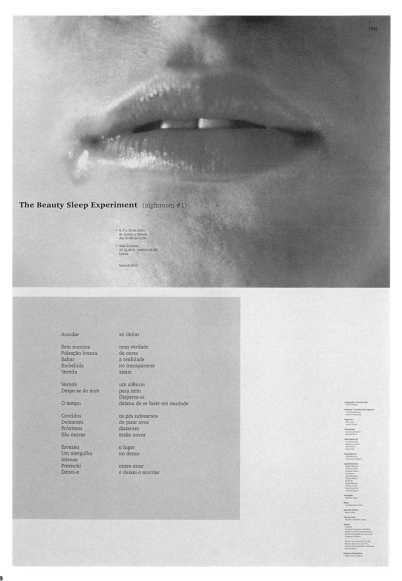

Book

Design_Lisa Hoffman
San Diego, California
Art Direction_Lisa Hoffman
Editors_Amanda Burt
and Summer Oram

Studio_Lisa Hoffman Design
Client_English Department,
California Polytechnic State
University, San Luis Obispo

Principal Type_Rosewood, Caslon
Book BE, Caslon Regular BE,
Minaret, and Byzantine

Dimensions_6 ½ x 8 ½ in.
(16.5 x 21.6 cm)

Brochure

Design_Tim Hagedorn
Bremen, Germany
Art Direction_Karsten Unterberger
Creative Direction_Almut Roeper
Project Manager_Sven Ruschek

Agency_in(corporate
communciation + design GmbH
Client_Lang + Schwarz
Wertpapierhandel AG

Principal Type_ITC Weidemann
and News Gothic

Dimensions_7 $^{11}/_{16}$ x 7 $^{11}/_{16}$ in.
(19.5 x 19.5 cm)

Brochure

Design_Joerg Bauer
Stuttgart, Germany
Art Direction_Joerg Bauer
Creative Direction_Reiner Hebe
and Joerg Bauer

Agency_HEBE Werbung + Design
Studio_Joerg Bauer Design
Client_HEBE Werbung + Design

Principal Type_Adobe Clarendon,
Trade Gothic, Leucadia, FB Magneto
Bold, FB Magneto Bold Extended,
and FB Magneto Super Bold

Dimensions_9⅝ x 11⅝ in.
(24.5 x 29.5 cm)

Poster

Design_Wang Xu
Guangzhou, China
Art Direction_Wang Xu
Creative Direction_Wang Xu

Studio_Wang Xu & Associates Ltd.
Client_Shanghai Graphic
Designers Association

Principal Type_Bauer Bodoni   **Dimensions**_23 ⅜ x 33 ¹⁄₁₆ in.
(59.4 x 84 cm)

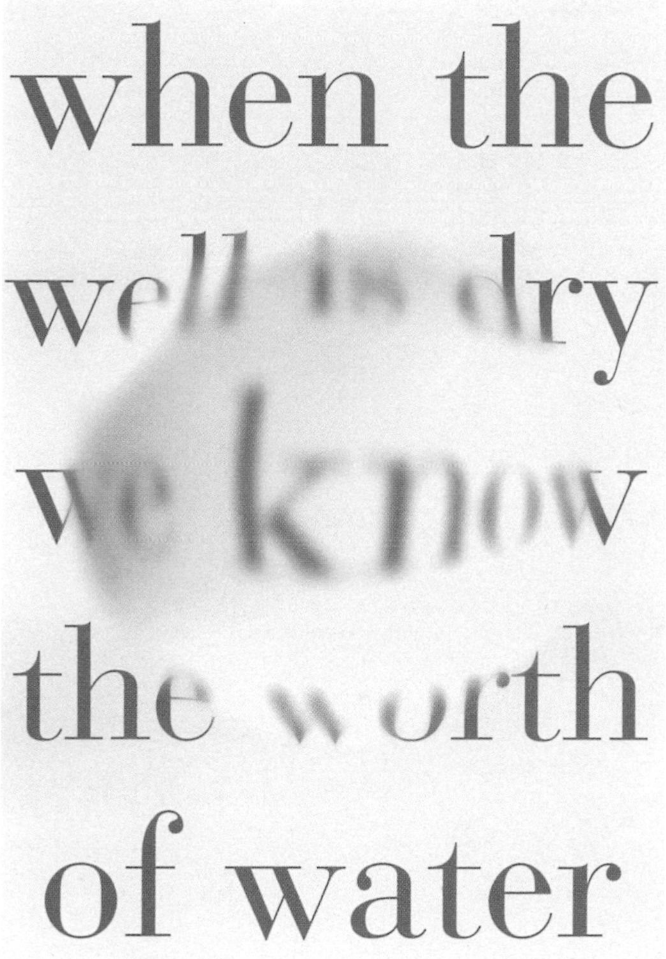

Poster

Design_David Beck Dallas, Texas
Lettering_Duane Michals
Art Direction_David Beck
Creative Direction_David Beck

Design Office_Sibley Peteet Design
Client_Dallas Society of
Visual Communications

Principal Type_Univers

Dimensions_22 x 30 in.
(55.9 x 76.2 cm)

Design_Bob Johnson
Sonoma, California
Lettering_Blair O'Neil
Art Direction_Bob Johnson
Creative Direction_Bob Broman
Printer_Dan Reimer Aurora Press

Agency_JohnsonLynch Advertising
Client_Bob Broman Winery

Principal Type_Goudy Handtooled
(modified)

Dimensions_1 ⅞ x 2 ¾ in.
(4.8 x 7 cm)

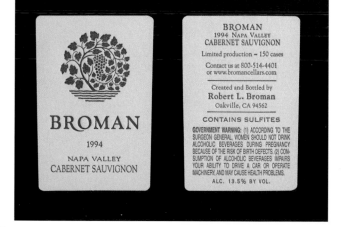

095

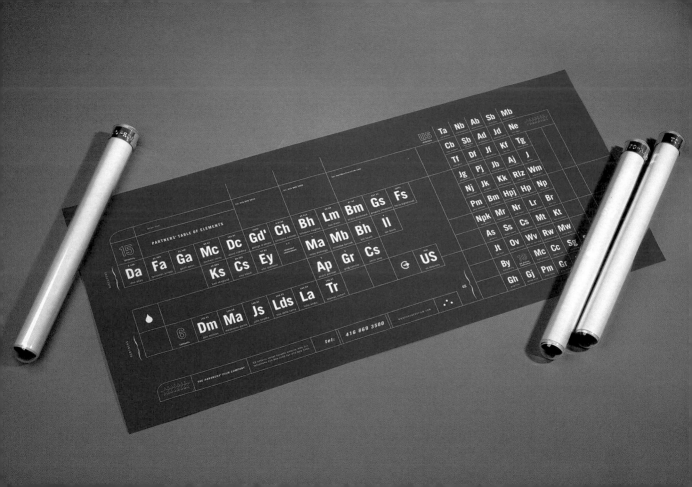

Design_Greg Lindy
Los Angeles, California
Art Direction_Greg Lindy
Creative Direction_Greg Lindy

Design Office_Intersection Studio
Client_School of Thought Records

Principal Type_Interstate and
Section

Dimensions_5 ¾ x 4 ¾ in.
(14.6 x 12.1 cm)

Design_Michael Bierut
and Nicole Trice
New York, New York
Art Direction_Michael Bierut

Design Office_Pentagram
Client_The Architectural League
of New York

Principal Type_Interstate Bold

Dimensions_23 ½ x 38 ½ in.
(59.7 x 97.8 cm)

Poster

Design_Norio Kudo Tokyo, Japan
Art Direction_Norio Kudo
Photography_Takahito Sato
Copywriter_Juri Sakuma

Design Office_Strike Co., Ltd.
Client_Japan Graphic Designers
Association, Inc.

Principal Type_Helvetica Bold

Dimensions_40 ⁹⁄₁₆ x 28 ⅝ in.
(103 x 72.8 cm)

Design_Joerg Bauer
and Jan Maier
Stuttgart, Germany
Art Direction_Joerg Bauer,
Jan Maier, and Nils Schubert
Photography_Nils Schubert
and Joerg Bauer

Design Office_Joerg Bauer Design
Client_Undercover

Principal Type_Cholla Unicase
Ligatures, Citizen, Dot Matrix,
Digital, Helvetica, and Helvetica
Neue Black

Dimensions_18 ⅛ x 24 in.
(46 x 61 cm)

Photography_ Headlight
Innovative Imagery
Copywriter_ Bianca Bohanan

Principal Type_ Arbitrary Sans,
Calvino Hand, and Keedy Sans

Dimensions_10 x 14 in.
(25.4 x 35.6 cm)

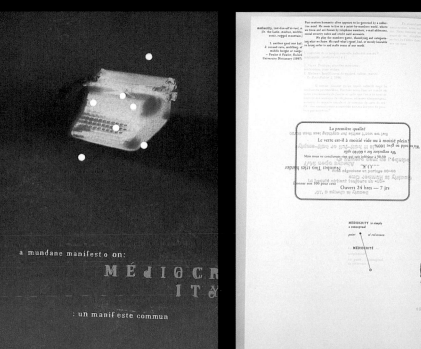

Design_Paula Scher
and Keith Daigle
New York, New York
Art Direction_Paula Scher

Design Office_Pentagram
Client_Metropolis

Principal Type_Trade Gothic

Dimensions_44½ x 31½ in.
(113 x 80 cm)

Design_Sibylle Reichelt
and Maike Truschkowski
Kassel, Germany
Photography_Werner Maschmann,
Constantin Meyer, Sibylle Reichelt,
and Maike Truschkowski

School_Kunsthochschule Kassel
Instructors_Christof Gassner
and Jörg Stürzebecher

Principal Type_Univers
Bold Condensed

Dimensions_15 ¾ x 11 ⅞ in.
(40 x 29.7 cm)

WHERE ARE YOU GOING?

K NOWING WHAT I'VE ...

WHAT IT IS

...

M⊙UTH

Smart Thinking

WHERE TO NEXT?

Wanting Against The Odds

SHE SAID, WHY NOT TRY IT THIS WAY, AND I SAID, WHY NOT

Jill Kuczmarski   1507 Mondler Avenue South Minneapolis, MN 55404

Date/Month/Year

Mr. or Ms. Addressee
Company Name
Street Address
City, State Zip Code

Dear Name of Addressee,

I was born in Rhinelander, Wisconsin. The world I grew up in was small but the energy was high. We lived on a farm, and aside from all the broken bones and emergency room visits, life was pretty quiet. Naturally, this has had an effect. In my case it has made me a risk taker, and has given me an understanding of how the beautiful can be useful, and vice versa.

The first time I remember noticing graphic design was helping my dad shop for tractor parts at Mill's Fleet Farm. I love all the images and objects at Fleet Farm, with its simple signage, packaging and layout. It really fertilizes the imagination (no pun intended). However, I actually made the decision to go into design as a career when I realized that design is one of the only professions where being strange is acceptable and I could talk about the aesthetic value of a beat-up Buick without the threat of being locked up in a padded room. Right now, my style tends toward the (underline one): conservative/exotic/classical/funky/ irreverent/other: delinquent Catholic schoolgirl.

This stationery system represents layers. On one hand it shows my passion for literature and old printed matter; on the other it represents my love for the eclectic. The only thing that was a given in this project was using French Paper. I chose Dur-O-Tone Newsprint Extra White because it is reminiscent of the vintage encyclopedias I used to ravish as a kid. Everything else was fill in the blank.

Since I am a little hard to follow at times, I would like to bring a certain clarity to my designs. I want to make people experience design, not just look at it. As for the future, I never want to grow up and I hope I can still be awed by at least two things a day until I die.

Sincerely,

Jill Kuczmarski
Design Student

Design_Masahiko Kimura
Tokyo, Japan
Art Direction_Masahiko Kimura

Client_Libreria Giannino Stoppani

Principal Type_Dante and
HonMincho

Dimensions_11⅝ x 8⅜ in.
(29.7 x 21.2 cm)

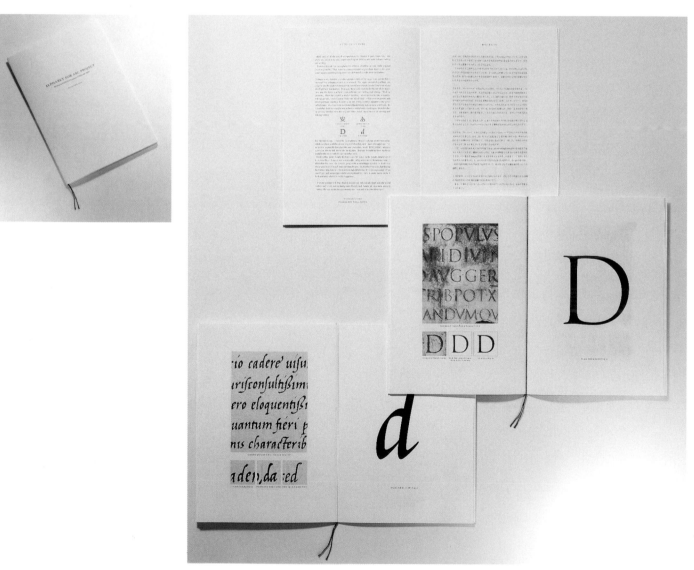

Design_Vittorio Costarella
Seattle, Washington
Lettering_Vittorio Costarella
Art Direction_Vittorio Costarella
Creative Direction_Mitch Nash

Studio_Modern Dog Design Co.
Client_Blue Q

Principal Type_Handlettering

Dimensions_2 ½ x 4 x 1¾ in.
(6.4 x 10.2 x 4.5 cm)

Packaging

Design_Douglas Dearden
Salt Lake City, Utah
Lettering_J. Otto Seibold
Art Direction_Douglas Dearden
Illustration_J. Otto Seibold

Design Office_AND
Client_Bink

Principal Type_Seibold and Courier

Dimensions_6 x 9 in.
(15.2 x 22.9 cm)

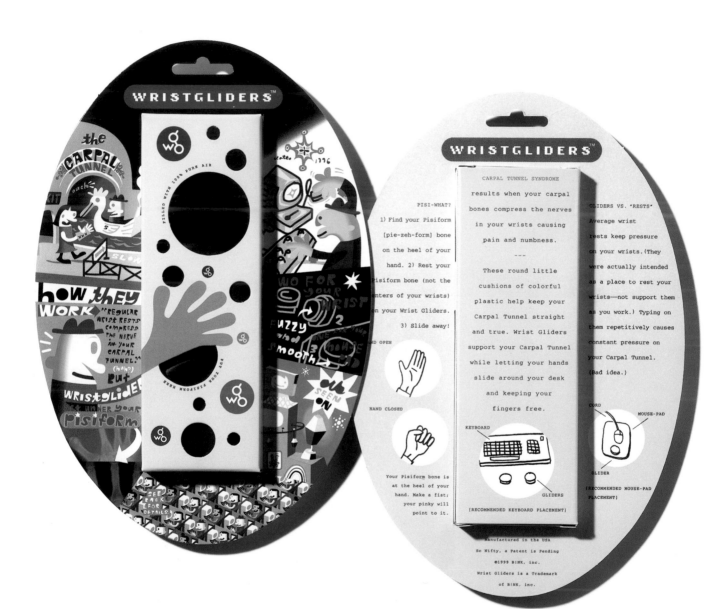

Design_David Plunkert
Baltimore, Maryland
Art Direction_David Plunkert

Design Office_SPUR Design LLC

Principal Type_Akzidenz Grotesk
and Shelley

Dimensions_4 ⅛ x 5 ¼ in.
(10.5 x 13.3 cm)

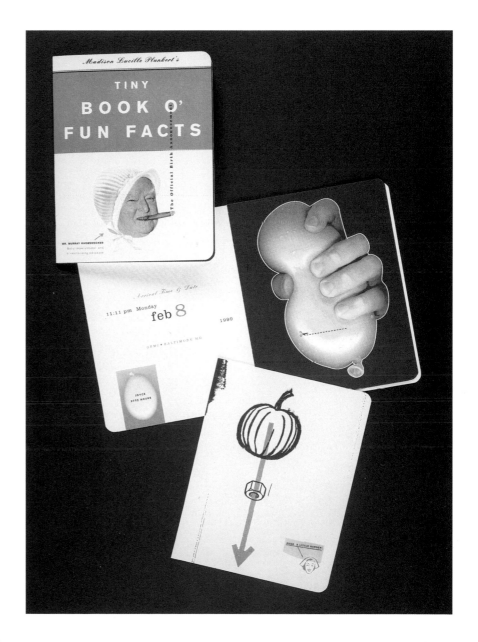

Design_Samantha Davenport
Atlanta, Georgia
Art Direction_David Cannon

Design Office_EAI
Client_Georgia Pacific Papers

Principal Type_ITC Franklin Gothic

Dimensions_6 x 8 in.
(15.2 x 20.3 cm)

WHAT'S 3 MINUTES?

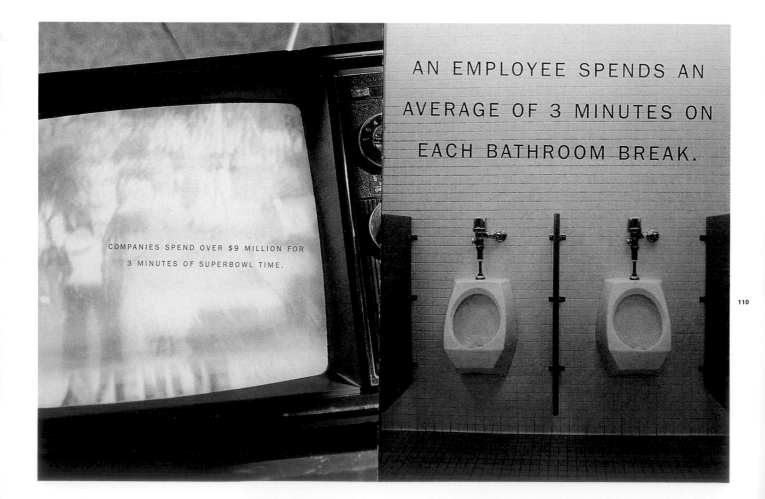

COMPANIES SPEND OVER $9 MILLION FOR
3 MINUTES OF SUPERBOWL TIME.

AN EMPLOYEE SPENDS AN
AVERAGE OF 3 MINUTES ON
EACH BATHROOM BREAK.

Design_Justyna Zareba
Passaic, New Jersey

School_School of Visual Arts
Instructor_James Victore

Principal Type_Zurich

Dimensions_6 x 9 in.
(15.2 x 22.9 cm)

111

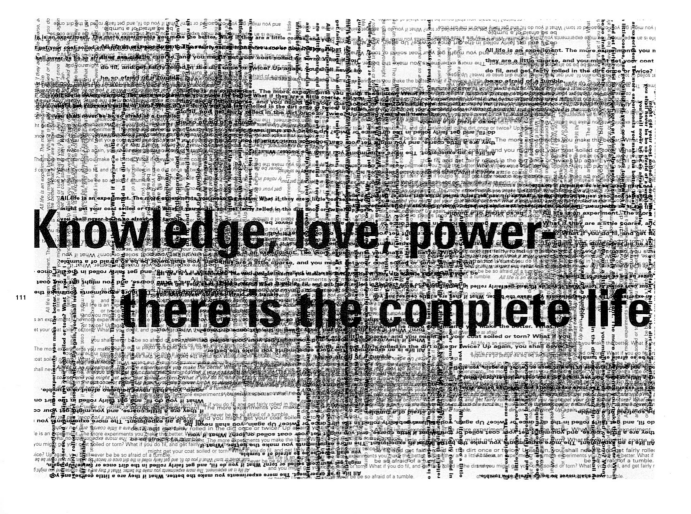

Design_Christian Toensmann
Hamburg, Germany

School_University for Applied
Science, Bielefeld
Instructor_Professor Gerd
Fleischmann

First Place

Principal Type_Trade Gothic Regular
and Monotype Baskerville Italic

Dimensions_8 ¹¹⁄₁₆ x 10 ⅝ in.
(22 x 27 cm)

Design_Mirko Ilić
New York, New York
Art Direction_Mirko Ilić

Studio_Mirko Ilić Corp.
Client_International Design Center

Principal Type_Based on Helvetica

Dimensions_27⅝ x 39⅜ in.
(70 x 100 cm)

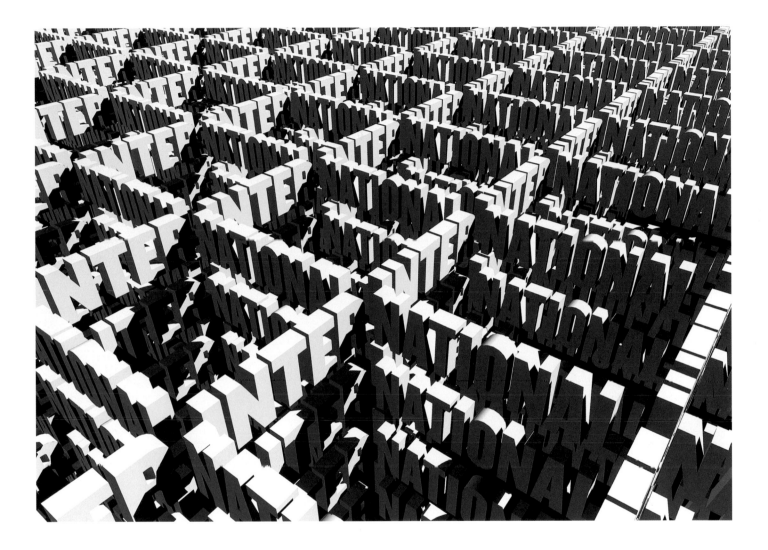

Design_Elizabeth Ackerman
New York, New York
Instructor_Carin Goldberg

School_School of Visual Arts

Principal Type_Trade Gothic

Dimensions_13 x 8 in.
(33 x 20.3 cm)

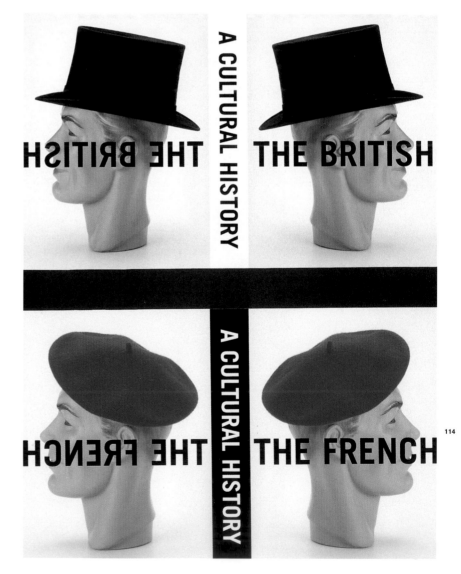

Design_Yoshiko Kusada
New York, New York
Instructor_L. Richard Poulin

Third Place

School_School of Visual Arts

Principal Type_Centaur

Dimensions_8 x 4 ¾ in.
(20.3 x 12.1 cm)

Facedown in ignorance Your mouths spilling words

Armed for slaughter.

The Rock cries out to us today,

You, created only a little lower than
The angels, have crouched too long in
The bruising darkness
Have lain too long

Here, on the pulse of this fine day
You may have the courage to look up and out and upon me,
The Rock, the River, the Tree, your country.
No less to Midas than the mendicant.
No less to you now than the mastodon then.

Here on the pulse of this new day
You may have the grace to look up and out
And into your sister's eyes,
And into your brother's face,

Your country,

and say simply very simply ——————— with hope

to say

the Asian
the Jew
the Native American
The Catholic
the French
The Irish
the Priest
The Gay
the Preacher
the homeless

The Creator gave to me when I and the Tree and the Rock were one.

the Hispanic
The African
the Sioux
the Muslim
the Greek
the Rabbi
the Sheik
the Straight
The privileged
the Teacher

Before cynicism was a bloody sear across your brow
And when you yet knew you still knew nothing.
The River sang and sings on.

There is a true yearning to respond to the singing River and the wise Rock.

They hear. They all hear the speaking of the Tree.

Design_S. Bogner
and A.M. Leslie
Munich, Germany
Art Direction_S. Bogner
Creative Direction_Factor Product
Collage_A.M. Leslie

Agency_Factor Product
Client_Häberlein & Mauerer
and Tony Stone

Principal Type_Space

Dimensions_23 ⅜
(59.4 x 84 cm)

W182×H226 28page, ALL COLOR
PRINT RUN 120,000 copies

PUBLISHED 5 and 20, PER MONTH

TOWER SPECIAL PICKS,
COMING SOON,
TOWER HIT CHART,
IN-STORE EVENT REPORT,
IN-STORE EVENT SCHEDULE,
WHAT'S HAPPENIN'?

TOWER RECORDS

f o r m

TOWER RECORDS INC.

NIHONSEIMEI SHIBUYA BLDG. 9F
1-21-1 JINNAN SHIBUYA-KU, TOKYO, JAPAN

u s i c

BRAHMAN COMPANY LIMITED

SHUWA MINAMI-AOYAMA RESIDENCE 504
2-22-4, MINAMI-AOYAMA MINATO-KU,
TOKYO, JAPAN

TOPPAN INC.

1-11-1 SHIMURA ITABASHI-KU,
TOKYO, JAPAN

l i f e

Principal Type_Lunatix
and Helvetica

Dimensions_60 x 35 in.
(23.6 x 88.9 cm)

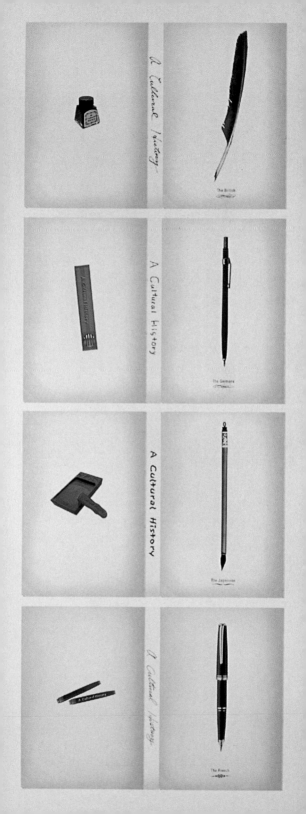

Design_Simone Mutert
Düsseldorf, Germany
Instructor_Prof. Helfried Hagenberg

Second Place

School_Fachhochschule Düsseldorf

Principal Type_Univers and Joanna **Dimensions**_Various

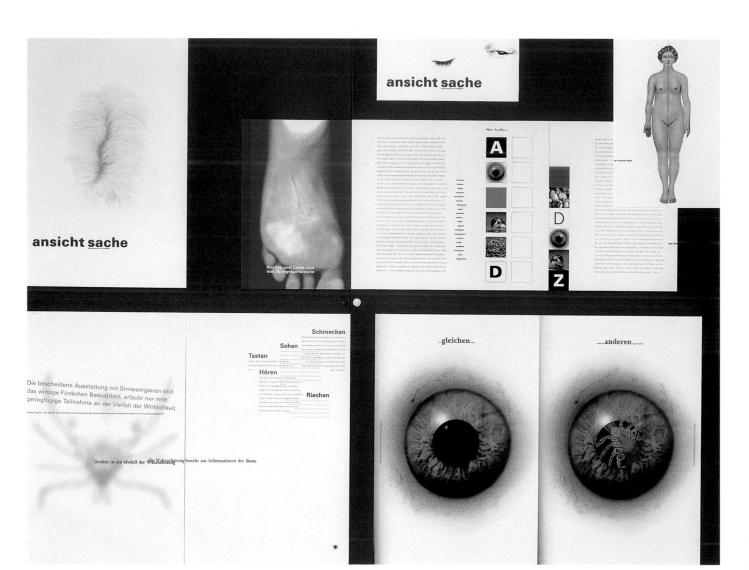

Design_Régine Thienhaus
Hamburg, Germany
Art Direction_Régine Thienhaus
Creative Direction_Prof.
Peter Wippermann
Photography_Nathanel Goldberg
and Claudia Kempf

Agency_Büro Hamburg JK.PW.
Client_Trendbüro B.K.W.

Principal Type_OCR Buero
and ITC Officina

Dimensions_8 ¼ x 11⁷⁄₁₆ in.
(21 x 29.7 cm)

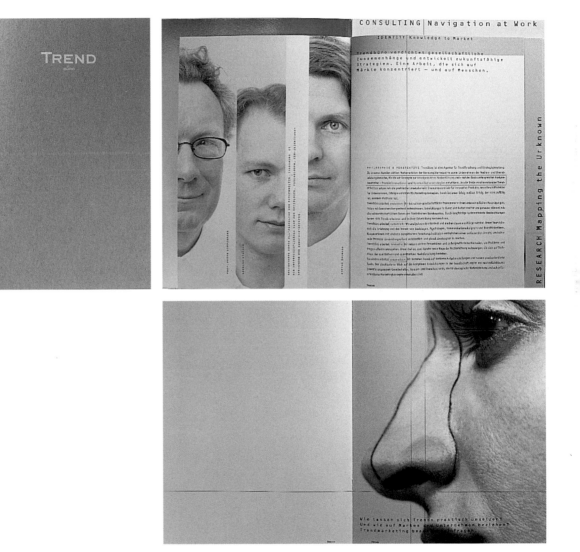

Design_Harry Pearce
Twickenham, England
Art Direction_Harry Pearce
and Domenic Lippa
Creative Direction_Harry Pearce
and Domenic Lippa

Studio_Lippa Pearce Design

Principal Type_AG Old Face,
HTF Champion Gothic, Didot,
and Bitstream Clarendon

Dimensions_8 ⅝ x 7 in.
(22 x 18 cm)

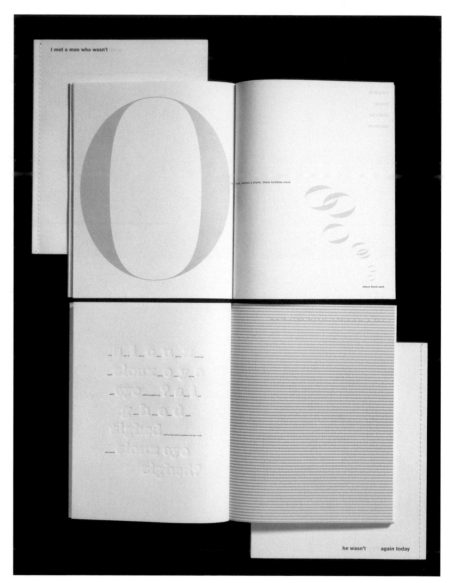

Poster

Design_Minao Tsukada
Tokyo, Japan
Art Direction_Minao Tsukada
Photography_Takahito Sato
Copywriter_Azusa Kajita

Studio_Strike Co., Ltd.

Principal Type_Morisawa MB 101

Dimensions_40 ⁵⁄₁₆ x 28 ⁵⁄₈ in.
(103 x 72.8 cm)

what needed to be done and how they needed to record their data. I told him I was ready to do it. Receiving the therapy was simple, not complicated at all. It wasn't uncomfortable or painful and best of all, I didn't have the depression, loss of appetite and hair loss that I had with chemotherapy.

They monitored me closely, collecting data every step of the way. Waiting in the hospital for results was the hardest part -- even though I actually felt shrinkage almost immediately. Because my tumors were on my ovaries, I actually felt the tumors shrinking inside me. I was told that other patients had similar kinds of experiences. With my first CT scan after I left the hospital, the doctor said it looked excellent and that they couldn't see tumors. There was scarring left over from the shrinkage of tumors, but the tumors were gone. I stayed in remission for five years.

In 1998, I had a feeling something was wrong because I could feel tightness in my throat. The doctor found a mass on the outside of my esophagus -- the cancer was back. Luckily, the tumors on my ovaries were still gone, but the cancer had found a new place in my body. I got the news of relapse, but my doctor said he'd treat me again. In June, I received another Bexxar treatment. So much progress had been made on the therapy, since my first treatment five years ago. It was like going to the doctor for a little procedure. First, they did blood work and all the preliminary pre-therapy steps, and then I had the treatment the same day. I was sent home without staying in the hospital overnight. Because of the radiation from the therapy, I shouldn't be around anyone for long periods of time for the first week. That was painless. I had scans to determine what the treatment had done. There was no tumor. Again, my lymphoma is gone. Now, I need to see my doctor every three months. When I'm in remission for a year, I'll only see him every six months. I feel fine.

I'm very thankful for this new drug which certainly helped me -- but my attitude helped me, too. I don't see things quite the same way. I try not to look in a negative way at things. We're all human and I'm no saint. But I realize I'll only be alive for a certain length of time and I really need to make the best of it while I'm here. Non-Hodgkin's lymphoma has made me realize that family and friends are most important in my life. I've been with my partner now for 10 years. He's been a real rock to lean on during this whole thing. When I talk to other non-Hodgkin's lymphoma patients, I tell them about this drug. I also tell them to keep a very positive attitude. Depend on the people that you love. No one can go through this alone. You need support.

GREAT JAZZ MUSIC IN THE SCULPTURE GARDEN AT THE SHELDON MEMORIAL ART GALLERY ADMISSION IS FREE MUSIC BEGINS AT 7PM JAZZ IN JUNE IS SPONSORED BY THE NEBRASKA ART ASSOCIATION CORPORATE FUNDING FROM NORWEST BANKS
JAZZ in June
Live Performance
Instrumental and Vocal
HOT SUMMERTIME GROOVE
(Every Tuesday Evening in June)
IRIE/The Gulizia Bros., June 02–Kevin Mahogany, June 09
Musa Nova, June 16–Bruce Katz, June 23
Ivan Paduart, June 30
57-60005
Made in U.S.A.
NOT LICENSED FOR RADIO BROADCAST
DEDICATED TO THE MEMORY OF KATHERINE FARREL MEDIA SPONSOR IS KFOR SPECIAL THANKS TO BAILEY LAUERMAN & ASSOC., NEBRASKA BUSINESS PRINTING, QUALI-GRAPHS, AND THE UNIVERSITY PROGRAM COUNCIL/UNL

Design_Darren Namaye
New York, New York
Art Direction_Darren Namaye
Creative Direction_Wendy Blattner

Design Office_Nuforia, Inc.
Client_Reebok International, Ltd.

Principal Type_MT News Gothic,
ITC New Baskerville, Rosewood,
and Eurostile

Dimensions_8 ¼ x 10 ¼ in.
(21 x 26 cm)

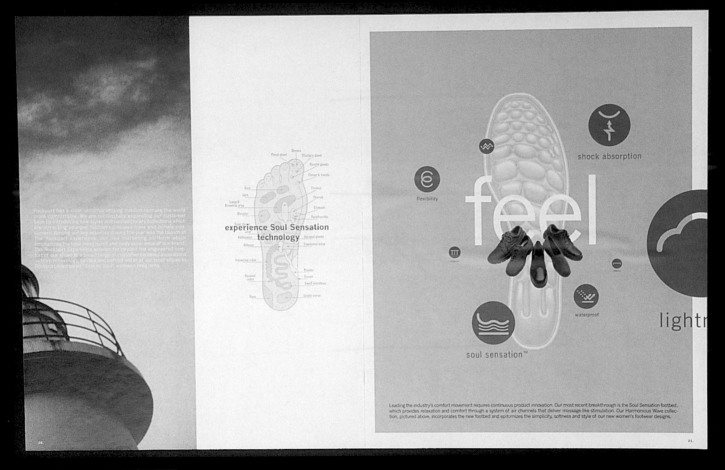

Design_Darren Namaye
New York, New York
Art Direction_Darren Namaye
Creative Direction_Wendy Blattner

Design Office_Nuforia, Inc.
Client_Reebok International, Ltd.

Principal Type_MT News Gothic,
ITC New Baskerville, Rosewood,
and Eurostile

Dimensions_8 ¼ x 10 ¼ in.
(21 x 26 cm)

Poster

Design_Ken Fox and Fletcher Martin
Chicago, Illinois
Creative Direction_Curtis Schreiber

Agency_VSA Partners
Client_Harley-Davidson
Motor Company

Principal Type_Bulmer, Adobe
Cheltenham, Adobe Century,
and BT Futura

Dimensions_20 x 35 in.
(50.8 x 88.9 cm)

Design_Giorgio Pesce
Lausanne, Switzerland
Art Direction_Giorgio Pesce
Creative Direction_Giorgio Pesce

Agency_Atelier Poisson
Client_Théâtre Arsenic

Principal Type_Triumvirate
and Trade Gothic

Dimensions_50⅜ x 35⁷⁄₁₆ in.
(128 x 90 cm)

129

Annual Report

Design_Todd Simmons
San Francisco, California
Art Direction_Bill Cahan
Creative Direction_Bill Cahan
Photography_Robert Schlatter
Illustration_Bill Barminski
Copywriter_Karen Langdon

Design Office_Cahan & Associates
Client_The Doctor's Company

Principal Type_Futura Heavy
Oblique and HTF Champion Gothic

Dimensions_6 ¼ x 9 in.
(15.9 x 2.9 cm)

Design_Katsuyuki Tanaka
Osaka, Japan
Art Direction_Katsuyuki Tanaka
Creative Direction_Katsuyuki Tanaka

Design Office_KPlant Co., Ltd.
Client_"S" Wonderland Co., Ltd.

Principal Type_Art Factory

Dimensions_40 ⁵⁄₁₆ x 28 ⁷⁄₁₆ in.
(103 x 72.8 cm)

Campaign

Design_Chris Froeter
Chicago, Illinois
Art Direction_Chris Froeter
Creative Direction_Chris Froeter

Design Office_Froeter Design Co., Inc.
Client_American Institute
of Graphic Arts/Chicago

Principal Type_Charcoal
and Bodoni

Dimensions_Various

Catalog

Design_Matt Eller and
Topher Sinkinson
Portland, Oregon
Creative Department_Alicia Johnson,
Matt Eller, Amie Champagne,
Kimberly Harrington, and
Topher Sinkinson
Creative Direction_Alicia Johnson
and Matt Eller

Production Team_Deborah Hyde
and Alan Foster
Design Firm_Johnson & Wolverton
Client_Photonica USA

Principal Type_Univers

Dimensions_9 x 11 ¾ in.
(22.9 x 30 cm)

Poster

Design_Takafumi Kusagaya
Tokyo, Japan
Art Direction_Takafumi Kusagaya

Design Office_Kusagaya Design, Inc.
Client_TGV Inc.

Principal Type_Custom

Dimensions_28 ⅛ x 40 ⅝ in.
(72.8 x 103 cm)

Brochure

Design_Sharon Werner
and Sarah Nelson
Minneapolis, Minnesota
Lettering_Todd ap Jones
Art Direction_Sharon Werner
Illustration_Allen Brewer,
Tom Garrett, Eric Hanson,
Dan Picasso, Elvis Swift,
Jack Molloy, and Joe Sorren

Design Studio_Werner Design
Werks, Inc.
Client_Joanie Bernstein, Art Rep

Principal Type_Adobe Clarendon,
Univers Extended, News Gothic,
and handlettering

Dimensions_10 x 12 in.
(25.4 x 30.5 cm)

Design_Patrick Bittner
and Isabel Bach
Saarbruecken, Germany
Art Direction_Patrick Bittner
Creative Direction_Ivica Maksimovic
Photography_Patrick Bittner and
Isabel Bach

Agency_Maksimovic & Partners
Client_Versorgungs – und
Verkehrsgesellschaft Saarbruecken

Principal Type_DIN Mittelschrift
and Engschrift

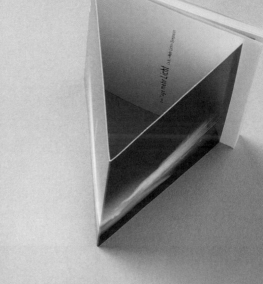

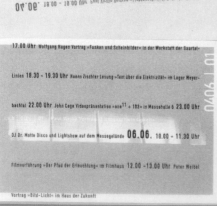

Design_Carolin Niemann
Düsseldorf, Germany
Art Direction_Klaus Hesse
Photography_Christian von
Alvensleben and Andreas Körner

Design Office_Hesse Designstudios
Client_Schemmrich

Principal Type_DIN Mittelschrift

Dimensions_8 ¼ x 7 ¼ in.
(21 x 18.3 cm)

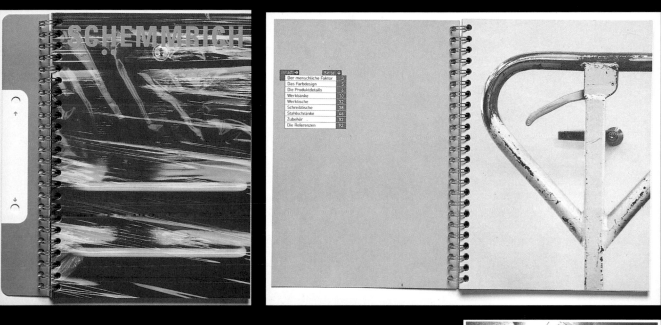

Design_Paul Sahre
New York, New York

Client_Rob Weisbach Books

Principal Type_HTF
Champion Gothic

Dimensions_20 x 30 in.
(50.8 X 76.2 cm)

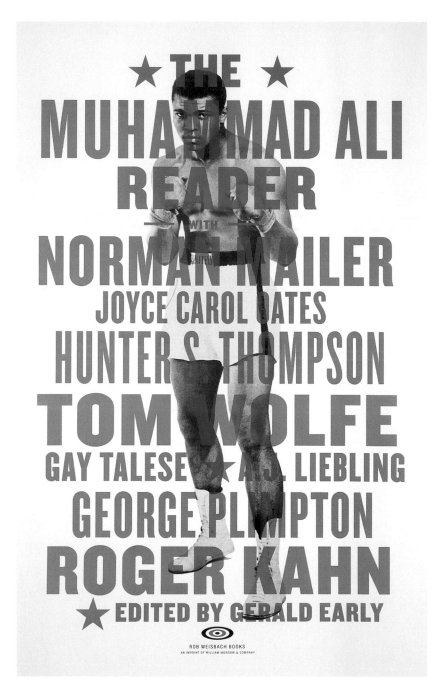

Catalog

Design_Peter Bain and Paul Shaw
Brooklyn, New York, and
New York, New York

Design Offices_Peter Bain Design
and Paul Shaw/Letter Design
Client_American Printing
History Association

Principal Type_Zentenar Fraktur,
Stempel Schneidler, and
Monotype Grotesque

Dimensions_7½ x 10½ in.
(19.1 x 26.7 cm)

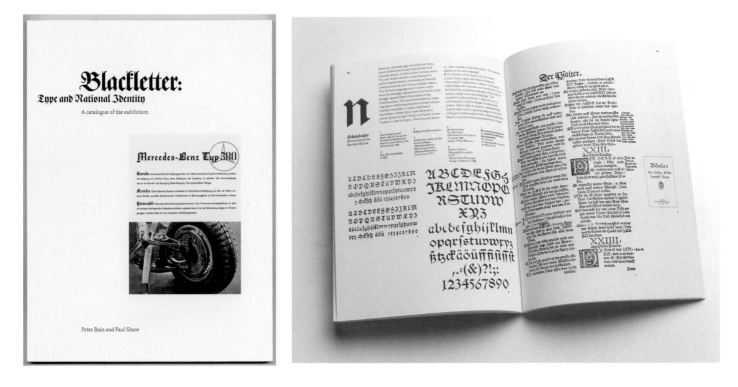

Design_Allison Williams,
Mats Hakansson, Yael Eisele,
Abby Clawson, and J.P. Williams
Art Direction_Allison Williams
Photography_Anita Calero

Studio_Design: M/W
Client_Takashimaya New York

Principal Type_Akzidenz Grotesk

Dimensions_7¼ x 9 in.
(18.4 x 22.9 cm)

Poster

Design_Claudia Schmauder
Zurich, Switzerland
Lettering_Claudia Schmauder
Art Direction_Claudia Schmauder
Creative Direction_Claudia
Schmauder

Client_Johann Jacobs Museum

Principal Type_Letters from
sales receipts, and screenshots

Dimensions_50 ⅜ x 35 ¼ in.
(128 x 89.5 cm)

Catalog

Design_ Vince Frost
London, England
Lettering_ Vince Frost
and Richard Rolf
Art Direction_ Vince Frost
Creative Direction_ Vince Frost
Printer_ House of Naylor

Studio_ Frost Design Ltd.
Client_4th Estate

Principal Type_ Wood and
metal type

Dimensions_5 ½ x 8 ½ in.
(14 x 21.6 cm)

Brochure

Design_Su Mathews
and JoJo Rhee
New York, New York
Art Direction_Michael Gericke
Photography_Peter Olsen
Copywriter_JoAnn Stone

Design Office_Pentagram
Client_Brooklyn Law School

Principal Type_HTF Hoefler
Engraved, Mrs. Eaves, and
Trade Gothic

Dimensions_12 x 7 in.
(30.5 x 17.8 cm

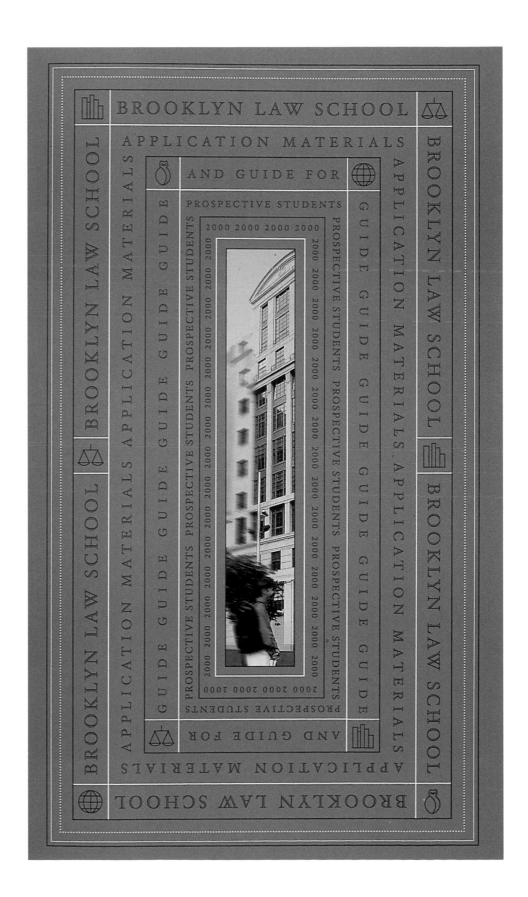

Poster

Design_Monica Peon
and Bob van Dÿk
The Hague, The Netherlands
Lettering_Bob van Dÿk

Agency_Studio Dumbar
Client_Zeebelt Theatre

Principal Type_Handlettering

Dimensions_23⅝ x 33⅛ in.
(60 x 80 cm)

Design_Mats Hakansson
New York, New York
Creative Direction_Allison Williams
and J. P. Williams

Studio_Design: M/W
Client_Champion International

Principal Type_Letter Gothic
and FF Scala Sans

Dimensions_5 x 6 ½ in.
(12.7 x 16.5 cm)

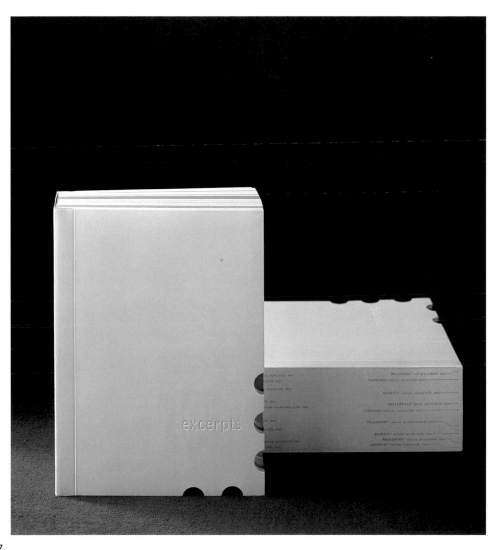

SiDEman

BLUE NIGHTS FATHERS SONS BURNING BRASS
THE NOTES BEND THE ERA ENDS THE MUSIC SURVIVES

Design_Thomas Leifer
and Judith Tielmann
Hamburg, Germany
Art Direction_Thomas Leifer

Design Office_Factor Design
Client_Hunzinger Information AG

Principal Type_Avenir BQ

Dimensions_16 %₁₆ x 9 ⅛₆ in
(42 x 23 cm)

Poster

Design_Olivier Sténuit,
Franck Sarfati, Joël Audenhaege
Brussels, Belgium
Art Direction_Olivier Sténuit,
Franck Sarfati, Joël Audenhaege
Creative Direction_Olivier Sténuit,
Franck Sarfati, Joël Audenhaege

Agency_[sign*]
Client_Encore Bruxelles

Principal Type_Akzidenz Grotesk

Dimensions_27⁹⁄₁₆ x 39³⁄₈ in.
(70 x 100 cm)

Design_Keiko Higashi
Osaka, Japan
Art Direction_Akio Okumura

Studio_Packaging Create Inc.
Client_Inter Medium Institute
Graduate School

Principal Type_Custom
and Univers

Dimensions_28 ¹¹⁄₁₆ x 40 ⁵⁄₁₆ in.
(72.8 x 103 cm)

Design_Akio Okumura
Osaka, Japan
Art Direction_Akio Okumura

Studio_Packaging Create Inc.
Client_Musa

Principal Type_Custom

Dimensions_7 ⅜ x 6 ¹⁵⁄₁₆ x 27 ⅜ in.
(18.8 x 17.4 x 69.5 cm)

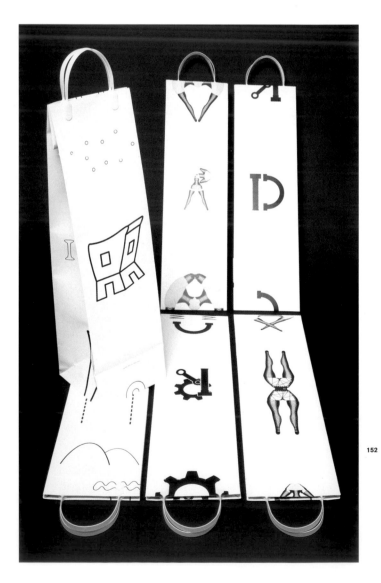

Design_Joe Scorsone
and Alice Drueding
Jenkintown, Pennsylvania
Art Direction_Joe Scorsone
and Alice Drueding

Design Office_Scorsone/Drueding

Principal Type_Monoline Script,
Schwere, and Franklin Gothic
Extra Condensed

Dimensions_30 ¹¹⁄₁₆ x 22 ¹³⁄₁₆ in.
(78 x 58 cm)

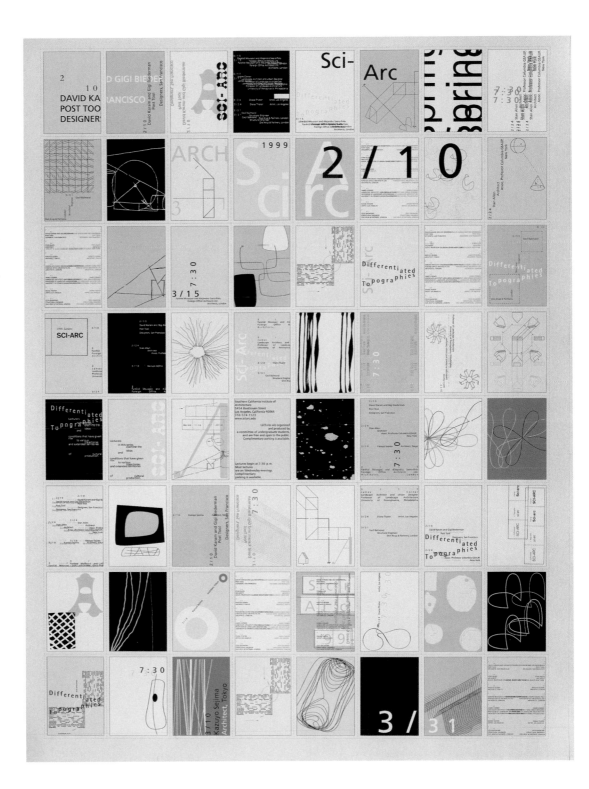

Poster

Design_Igors Irbe and Inguna Irbe
Chicago, Illinois
Art Direction_Inguna Irbe
Creative Direction_Igors Irbe
Photography_Maria Astrid Gonzales

Studio_Irbe Design

Principal Type_Orator,
Letter Gothic, and FF Bodoni

Dimensions_8 ½ x 11 in.
(21.6 x 27.9 cm)

Design_Charles S. Anderson,
Todd Piper-Hauswirth,
and Kyle Hames
Art Direction_Charles S. Anderson
Illustration_Charles S. Anderson
and Kyle Hames
Copywriter_Lisa Pemrick

Design Office_Charles S.
Anderson Design
Client_French Paper Company

Principal Type_Trade Gothic
and Univers

Dimensions_18 ½ x 25 in.
(47 x 63.5 cm)

Principal Type_Univers
Black Extended

Dimensions_14 x 2 in.
(35.6 x 55.9 cm)

COLUMBIA ARTISTS AND ARIELLE TEPPER PRESENT TRAINSPOTTING ADAPTED BY HARRY GIBSON
FROM THE NOVEL BY IRVINE WELSH WITH TESSA AUBERJONOIS DARA COLEMAN SEBASTIAN ROCHÉ SETH ULLIAN
SET DESIGNER JOE ROBINSON LIGHTING DESIGNER JEFFREY KOGER COSTUME DESIGNER JULIE ROBBINS SOUND DESIGNER RAYMOND D. SCHILKE
CASTING JAY BINDER & ASSOC./AMY KITTS PRESS REPRESENTATION THE PUBLICITY OFFICE MARKETING THE KARPEL GROUP

PRODUCTION STAGE MANAGER CHRISTINE CATTI PRODUCTION SUPERVISOR PROGRESSIVE PROD. GENERAL MANAGER PAUL MORER
EXECUTIVE PRODUCER ALDO SCROFANI DIRECTED BY HARRY GIBSON ORIGINAL LONDON AND U.K. PRODUCTIONS PRODUCED BY G & J PRODUCTIONS LTD. AND DONNA KNIGHT

PLAYERS THEATRE 115 MacDOUGAL STREET

keshi kaneshiro Charlie young Michele Reis Karen Mok

The guideline I gave my designer Wing on the poster of HAPPY TOGETHER was a story about two people. After trying various layouts, from First to Second and Tango to Smoking, I realized the two people were getting closer and closer. Finally, we settled on the most direct image and changed the title to HAPPY TOGETHER.

ATOMIC ENERGY

LAND SPECULATION · VINEY
FARMERS MINING TOWNS CH
WOODS HARBORS INLAND WATERW
OVEMENT OPERA HOUSE NATURALIS
EL ISLAND · ASIAN EXCLUSION ACTS

158

Hello,
my
name
is
BRAHMAN.
I
was
born
in
Tokyo
in
1997.
Remember
me,
please.
Thanks
a lot.

BRAHMAN COMPANY LIMITED
SHUWA MINAMI-AOYAMA RESIDENCE 504
3-23-4, MINAMI-AOYAMA MINATO-KU, TOKYO, JAPAN

ARSENIC

L'ARRIVISTE

Texte Stig Dagerman   Mise en scène Martine Charlet

Du 11 au 23 janvier 2000

289.–

 matinées à 18h00 (mer à 20h30 di à 17h00
(di avec service de garderie gratuit sur réservation)

ARSENIC
Rue de Genève 57, 1004 Lausanne

PRIX DES PLACES
Plein tarif: Fr 28.-/14.-*
Tarif réduit (app, étu, AVS-AI, chô): Fr 18.-/9.-*

RESERVATIONS
021-625 11 36   http://www.cyberlab.ch/arsenic

* avec notre abonnement demi-tarif

La Fondation de l'Arsenic bénéficie du soutien de
la Ville de Lausanne et de l'Etat de Vaud

PRO HELVETIA

CyberLAB

Stationery

Design_Kevin Krueger
Dundee, Illinois
Art Direction_Kevin Krueger
and Greg Samata
Creative Direction_Kevin Krueger
and Greg Samata

Design Office_SamataMason
Client_Candace Gelman
& Associates

Principal Type_Bembo

Dimensions_6 x 8¼ in.
(15.3 x 21 cm)

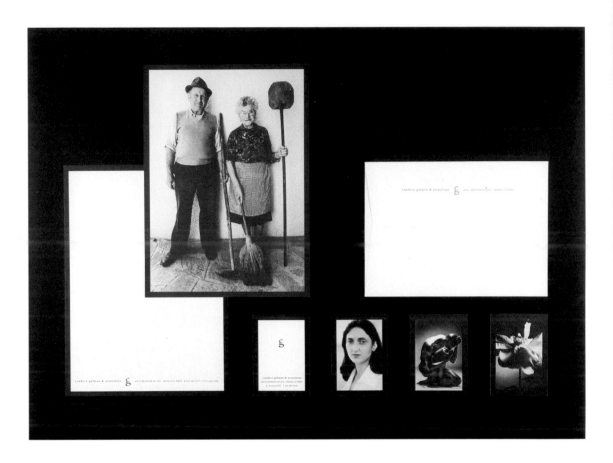

Design_Darren Namaye
New York, New York
Art Direction_Darren Namaye
Creative Direction_Darren Namaye,
Loid Der, and Brenna Garratt

Design Office_Nuforia, Inc.
Client_Exult

Principal Type_Univers Extended
and Univers

Dimensions_13 x 19¾ in.
(33 x 50.2 cm)

Student Work

Design_Justin Salvas
Woodstock, Connecticut
Instructor_Valerie Wagner

School_School of Visual Arts

Principal Type_Gothic 13   **Dimensions**_18 x 24 in.
                                   (45.7 x 61 cm)

Design_Effendy Wijaya
New York, New York
Instructor_Carin Goldberg

School_School of Visual Arts

Principal Type_Futura Stencil

Dimensions_24 x 32 in.
(61 x 81.3 cm)

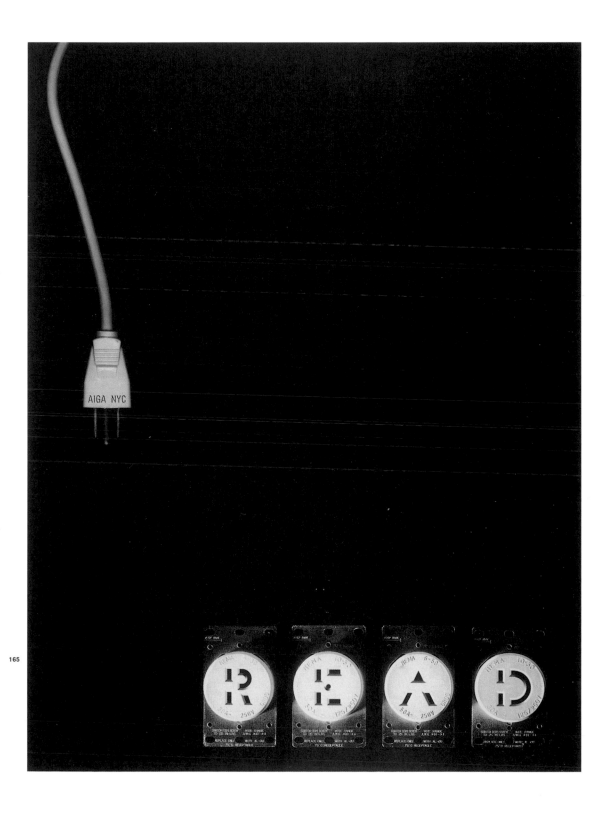

Student Work

Design_Second-year
photography students
Art Direction_Ritva Leinonen
and Sakari Nenye

School_Lahti Polytechnic
Institute of Design
Lahti, Finland

Principal Type_Mrs. Eaves   **Dimensions**_6 ⅜ x 5 ⁹⁄₁₆ in.
(16.2 x 14.2 cm)

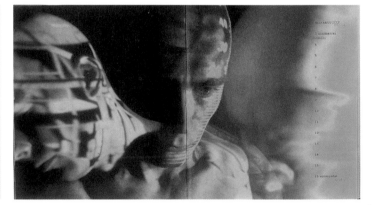

Design_Will de l'Ecluse,
Hans Bockting, and David Smith
Amsterdam, The Netherlands
Photography_André Thijssen
Typographers_Will de l'Ecluse
and David Smith

Design Office_UNA (Amsterdam)
designers
Client_Stichting Educatieve
Omroep Teleac/NOT

Principal Type_Trinité

Dimensions_9¼ x 12⁹⁄₁₆ in.
(23.5 x 32 cm)

Calendar

Design_Susie Stampley
Richardson, Texas
Art Direction_Stephen Zhang
Creative Direction_Tim Hale
and Kosta Kartsotis

Studio_Fossil Design Studio

Principal Type_Interstate
and ITC Officina

Dimensions_5½ x 6½ in.
(14 x 16.5 cm)

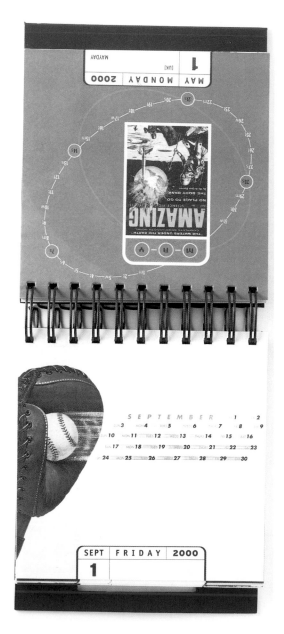

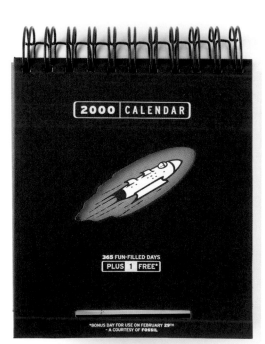

Calendar

Design_John Pylypczak
Toronto, Canada
Art Direction_Diti Katona and
John Pylypczak, Larry Gaudet
Printer_C.J. Graphics
Printers & Lithographers

Studio_Concrete Design
Communications

Principal Type_New Clarendon

Dimensions_6 ¾ x 7 ¼ in.
(17.2 x 18.4 cm)

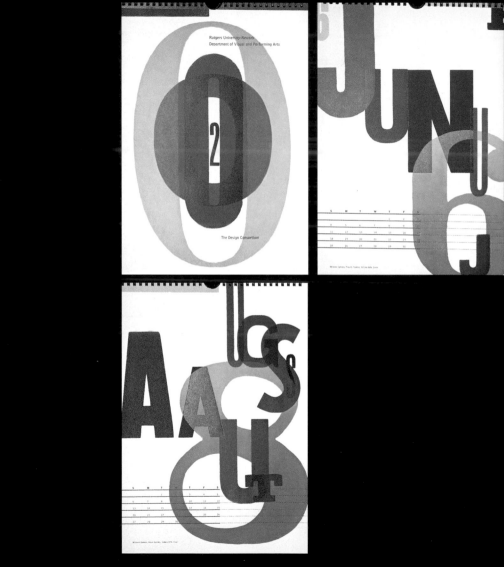

Design_Jason Schulte
Minneapolis, Minnesota
Art Direction_Charles S. Anderson
Copywriter_Lisa Pemrick

Design Office_Charles S.
Anderson Design
Client_French Paper Company

Principal Type_Custom

Dimensions_19 x 25 in.
(48.3 x 63.5 cm)

Design_ Jun Takechi
Tokyo, Japan
Art Direction_ Jun Takechi
Copywriter_ Hideyuki Sekikawa

Design Office_ Jun Takechi
Client_ The Kuricorder Foundation

Principal Type_ Custom

Dimensions_40⁹⁄₁₆ x 28¹⁵⁄₁₆ in.
(103 x 72.8 cm)

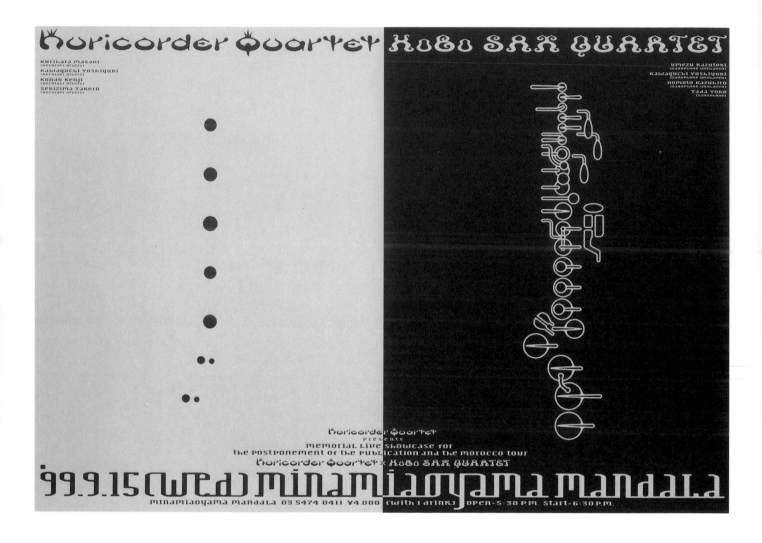

Poster

Design_Akihiko Tsukamoto
Tokyo, Japan
Art Direction_Akihiko Tsukamoto
Printer_Twin-Eight Co., Ltd.

Studio_Zuan Club
Client_DIG Tokyo Corporation

Principal Type_Kabello Extra Bold
and Gill Sans Extra Bold

Dimensions_28¹¹⁄₁₆ x 40⁹⁄₁₆ in.
(72.8 x 103 cm)

Design_Traci Code
Chicago, Illinois
Art Direction_Robert Petrick
Creative Direction_Robert Petrick
Photography_Jeff Stephens

Design Office_Petrick Design
Client_Ivex Packaging Corporation

Principal Type_ITC Franklin Gothic

Dimensions_8 ¾ x 11 ¾ in.
(22.2 x 29.8 cm)

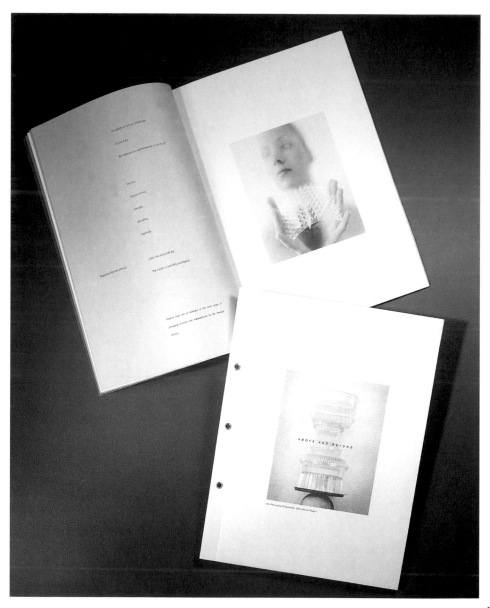

Design_Stephen Zhang
Richardson, Texas
Art Direction_Tim Hale,
Casey McCarr and Stephen Zhang
Creative Direction_Tim Hale
Illustration_Ellen Tanner,
John Vineyard, Susie Stampley,
Paula Wallace, Jennifer Burk,
and Andrea Haynes

Design Studio_Fossil Design Studio

Principal Type_Base
and Mrs. Eaves

Dimensions_7 ½ x 11 in.
(19 x 27.9 cm)

Design_Vince Frost
London, England
Art Direction_Vince Frost
Creative Direction_Vince Frost
Printer_Artomatic

Studio_Frost Design Ltd.
Client_Chartered Society
of Designers

Principal Type_Wood type

Dimensions_28½ x 40 in.
(72.4 x 101.6 cm)

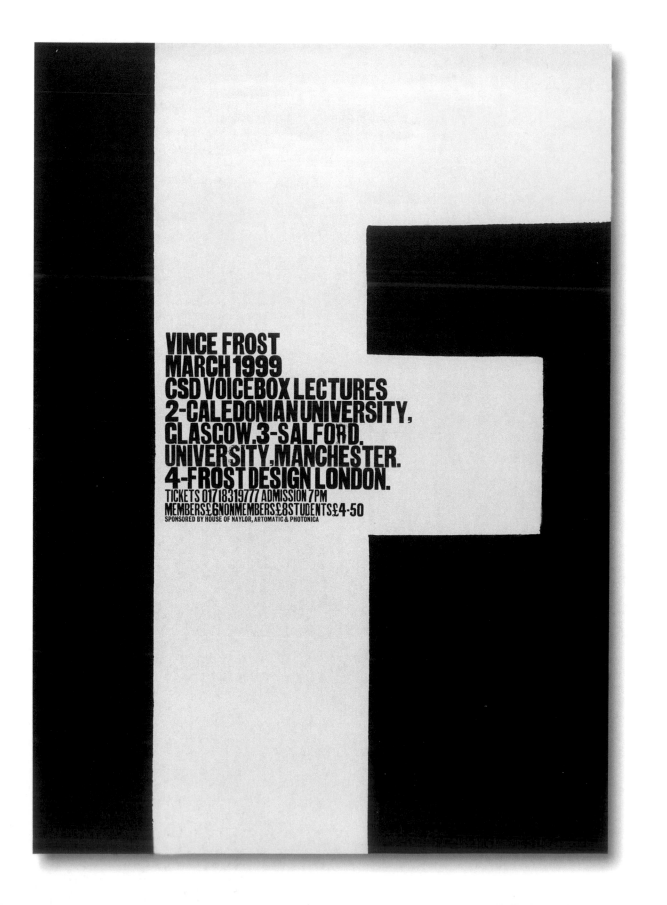

Annual Report

Design_Jennifer Sterling
San Francisco, California
Art Direction_Jennifer Sterling
Creative Direction_Jennifer Sterling
Illustration_Jennifer Sterling
and Amy Hayson

Design Office_Jennifer Sterling
Design
Client_DSP

Principal Type_Frutiger,
Garamond No. 3, and handlettering

Dimensions_6 ¾ x 9 ¾ in.
(17.2 x 24.8 cm)

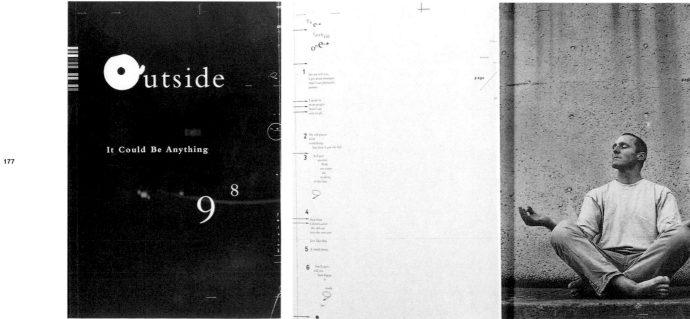

Design_Theresa Kwan
Toronto, Canada
Art Direction_Diti Katona
and John Pylypczak
Illustration_Arendas Josef
Printer_C.J Graphics
Printers & Lithographers

Studio_Concrete Design
Communications
Client_The Design Exchange

Principal Type_Trade Gothic

Dimensions_24 x 36 in.
(61 x 91.4 cm)

Design_Marion English Powers
Birmingham, Alabama
Art Direction_Marion English Powers
Creative Direction_Terry Slaughter
and Marion English Powers

Agency_Slaughter Hanson
Client_Greater Alabama Council

Principal Type_Alternate Gothic,
Bell Gothic, and Caslon 540

Dimensions_8 ¾ x 11½ in.
(22.2 x 29.2 cm)

FOR CLOSE TO A CENTURY, SCOUTING HAS HELPED BOYS REALIZE THEIR OWN POTENTIAL, SHOWING THEM THE GREATNESS THAT IS WITHIN THEIR GRASP. SCOUTS LEARN THAT, NO MATTER WHO THEY ARE, NO MATTER WHAT THEIR CIRCUMSTANCES, THEY TOO ARE CAPABLE OF MAKING A POSITIVE IMPACT ON THE WORLD. SCOUTING HAS SHAPED THEIR CHARACTER, INSTILLING TRAITS THAT WILL LEAD THEM TO DO EXTRAORDINARY THINGS. FOR THESE INDIVIDUALS, INCLUDING THE FIVE PROFILED IN THIS ANNUAL REPORT, SCOUTING HAS BECOME A HANDBOOK FOR LIFE. A HANDBOOK FOR CHARACTER.

Electronic

Design_Winnie Tan
Singapore
Art Direction_Winnie Tan
Creative Direction_Winnie Tan

Studio_Nimbus Design

Principal Type_Gill Sans
and Bitstream Arrus

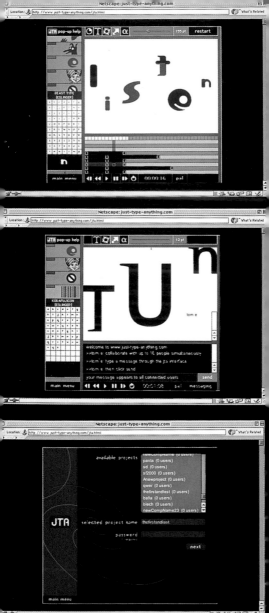

Design_Sayuri Shoji
a   elson Wong
New York, New York
Art Direction_Sayuri Shoji
Programmer/Sound_Antonio Cruz

Studio_Sayuri Studio
Client_Issey Miyake

Principal Type_Helvetica Neue

Interactive Media

Design_Sam Davy, David Eveleigh,
and Frances Jackson
London, England
Creative Direction_Tim Fendley
Programmer_David Eveleigh
Technical Director_Andreas Harding

Agency_MetaDesign London
Client_Glasgow 1999: UK City
of Architecture and Design

Principal Type_Glasgow 1999

Design_Dominik Mycielski
Köln, Germany

School_Fachhochschule Düsseldorf
Instructors_Professor Phillip Teufel
and Stefan Nowak

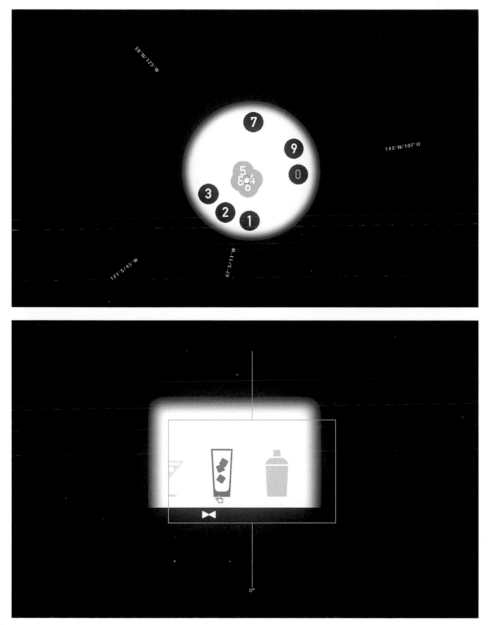

Stationery

Design_Anuthin Wongsunkakon
Bangkok, Thailand
Art Direction_Anuthin Wongsunkakon

Studio_Graphic Behaviour

Principal Type_Son Gothic

Dimensions_8½ x 11 in.
(21.6 x 27.9 cm)

Design_David Plunkert
Baltimore, Maryland
Art Direction_David Plunkert

Design Office_SPUR Design LLC

Principal Type_Akzidenz Grotesk   **Dimensions**_8 ½ x 11 in.

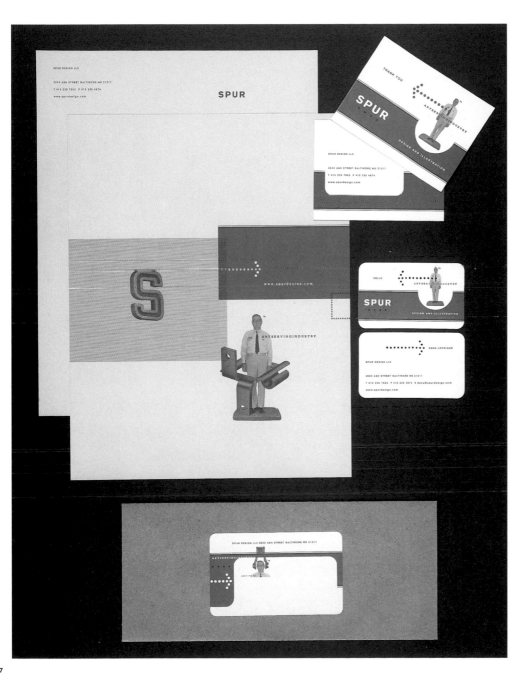

Corporate Communications

Design_Brian Diecks
and Amanda Hayes
New York, New York
Creative Direction_Brian Diecks
Animation_Dana Schecter
Editor_Chris O'Neil
Producer_Eve Ehrich

Agency_McCann Erickson, Detroit
Design Office_The Diecks Group, Inc.
Client_Buick

Principal Type_Beta Sans Oblique

Design_Clive Piercy and
Carol Kono
Santa Monica, California
Art Direction_Clive Piercy
and Michael Hodgson

Design Office_Ph.D
Client_Foundation Press

Principal Type_Various

Dimensions_2 ⅛ x 3 ⅜ in.
(5.4 x 8.6 cm)

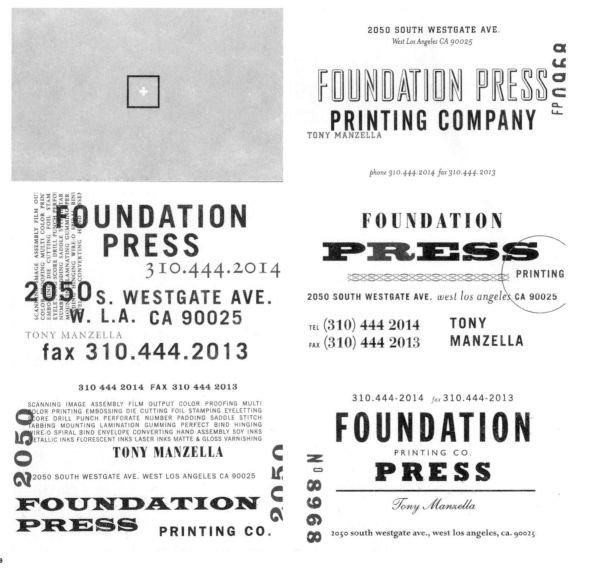

Design_Rishi Shourie
San Francisco, California
Art Direction_Rishi Shourie
and Mikon Van Gastel
Creative Direction_Brian Bacino,
Steve Fong, Dann Wilkens,
and Kyle Cooper
Writer_Dann Wilkens

Agency_Foote, Cone & Belding
Studio_Imaginary Forces
Client_Sega Dreamcast

Principal Type_DIN Mittelschrift
and Sackers Gothic

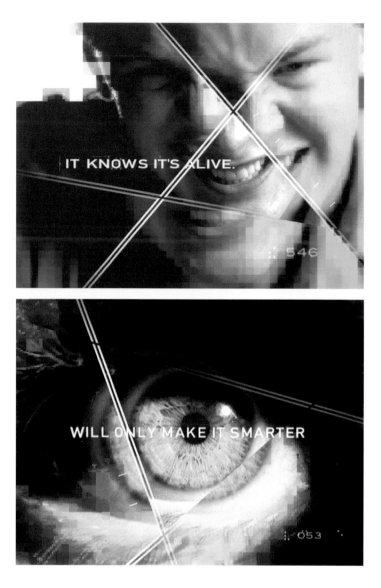

Design_Richard Boynton
Minneapolis, Minnesota
Art Direction_Richard Boynton
Creative Direction_Richard Boynton

Design Office_Wink
Client_Push

Principal Type_Eurostile Extended
and Bubbledot

Dimensions_8 ½ x 11 in.
(21.6 x 27.9 cm)

ELXR:DSGN

2134 VAN NESS AVE. SAN FRANCISCO, CA 94109 TEL 415-834-0300 FAX 415-834-0101

DESIGNER: ND@ELIXIRDESIGN.COM

JENNIFER JERDE
DAVID CASO
NATHAN DURRANT
HOLLY HOLMQUIST
JENNIFER TOLO
MEREL KENNEDY
KYLE PIERCE
ERIC HEIMAN

CREATIVE DIRECTOR: JJ@ELIXIRDESIGN.COM

DAVID CASO
NATHAN DURRANT
JENNIFER TOLO
MEREL KENNEDY
HOLLY HOLMQUIST
JENNIFER JERDE
KYLE PIERCE
ERIC HEIMAN

GENERAL MANAGER: KP@ELIXIRDESIGN.COM

HOLLY HOLMQUIST
JENNIFER JERDE
DAVID CASO
NATHAN DURRANT
KYLE PIERCE
MEREL KENNEDY
JENNIFER TOLO
ERIC HEIMAN

DESIGNER: HH@ELIXIRDESIGN.COM

KYLE PIERCE
JENNIFER TOLO
JENNIFER JERDE
NATHAN DURRANT
HOLLY HOLMQUIST
DAVID CASO
MEREL KENNEDY
ERIC HEIMAN

DESIGNER: JT@ELIXIRDESIGN.COM

DAVID CASO
NATHAN DURRANT
MEREL KENNEDY
JENNIFER TOLO
HOLLY HOLMQUIST
KYLE PIERCE
JENNIFER JERDE
ERIC HEIMAN

DESIGNER: MK@ELIXIRDESIGN.COM

DAVID CASO
NATHAN DURRANT
JENNIFER TOLO
MEREL KENNEDY
HOLLY HOLMQUIST
JENNIFER JERDE
KYLE PIERCE
ERIC HEIMAN

Design_Stefan Sagmeister
New York, New York
Lettering_Stefan Sagmeister
and Hjalti Karlsson
Art Direction_Stefan Sagmeister
Creative Direction_Stefan Sagmeister

Design Office_Sagmeister Inc.
Client_Anni Kuan Design

Principal Type_Franklin Gothic
Demi and handlettering

Dimensions_3 ½ x 2 in.
(8.9 x 5.1 cm)

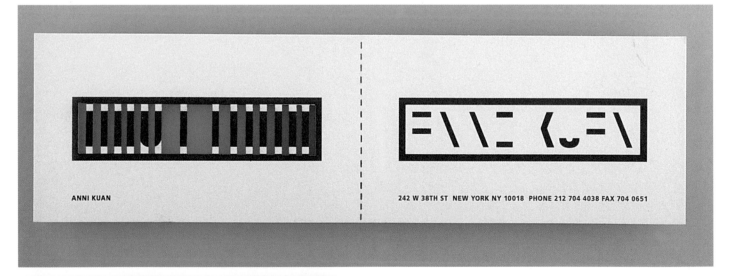

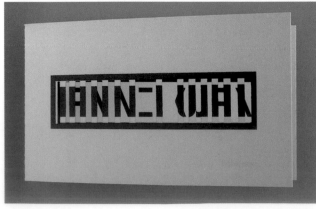

Television Commercial

Design_Matt Cullen
and Mikon van Gastel
Hollywood, California
Executive Production_Saffron Kenny
Production_Lisa Laubhan (IF)
and Jill Andresevic (Agency)
Art Direction_Mikon van Gastel
and Alain Briere
Creative Direction_Peter Frankfurt

Editor_Adrian Kays
Inferno Artist_Marijose Auclair
Directon_Matt Cullen
and Mikon van Gastel
2nd Animation_Matt Cullen
Coordinator_Keith Bryant
Voice-over_Henry Rollins
Agency_J. Walter Thompson
Design Office_Imaginary Forces

Client_Unicef and Merrill Lynch
Principal Type_FF DIN Alternate

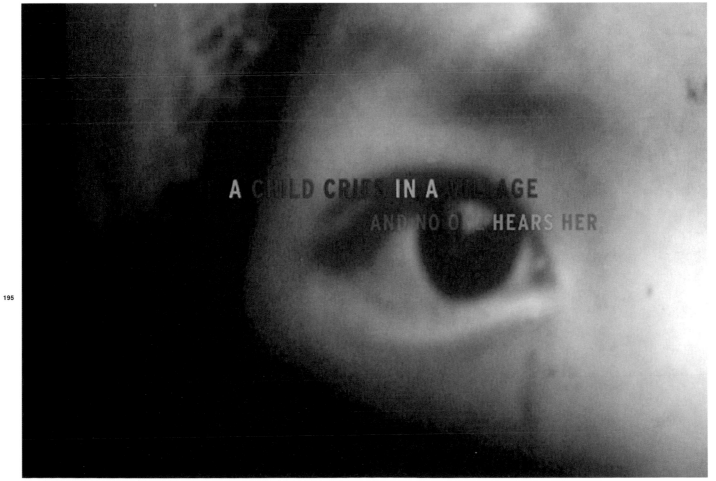

Annual Report

Design_Joyce Nesnadny
and Michelle Moehler
Cleveland, Ohio
Art Direction_Mark Schwartz
and Joyce Nesnadny
Photography_Stephen Frailey

Design Office_Nesnadny
+ Schwartz
Client_The Progressive Corporation

Principal Type_Interstate

Dimensions_8 ½ x 11 in.
(21.6 x 27.9 cm)

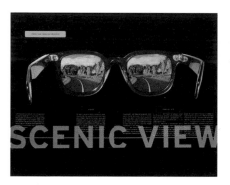

Annual Report

Design_Ted Bluey
San Francisco, California
Art Direction_David Salanitro
Creative Direction_David Salanitro
Photography_Hunter L. Wimmer

Design Office_Oh Boy,
A Design Company
Client_Robertson-Ceco Corporation

Principal Type_Helvetica Neue
Medium and Univers

Dimensions_11 x 17 in.
(27.9 x 43.2 cm)

Corporate Identity

Design_Yasuyo Fukumoto
Osaka, Japan
Art Direction_Akio Okumura

Studio_Packaging Create Inc.
Client_Japan Bridge

Principal Type_Custom

Dimensions_11 ¹¹⁄₁₆ x 8 ¼ in.
(29.7 x 21 cm)

Corporate Identity

Design_Akio Okumura
Osaka, Japan
Art Direction_Akio Okumura

Studio_Packaging Create Inc.
Client_Inter Medium Institute
Graduate School

Principal Type_Custom
Tomohiro Tokimoto

Dimensions_13 x 9 ⁷⁄₁₆ in.
(33.2 x 24 cm)

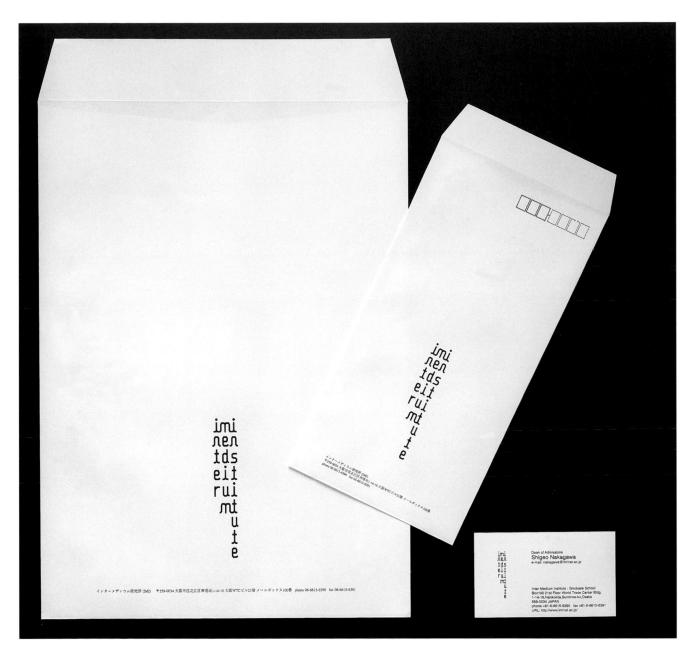

Corporate Identity

Design_Yasuyo Fukumoto
Osaka, Japan
Art Direction_Akio Okumura

Studio_Packaging Create Inc.
Client_Japan Bridge

Principal Type_Custom

Dimensions_11¹¹⁄₁₆ x 8¼ in.
(29.7 x 21 cm)

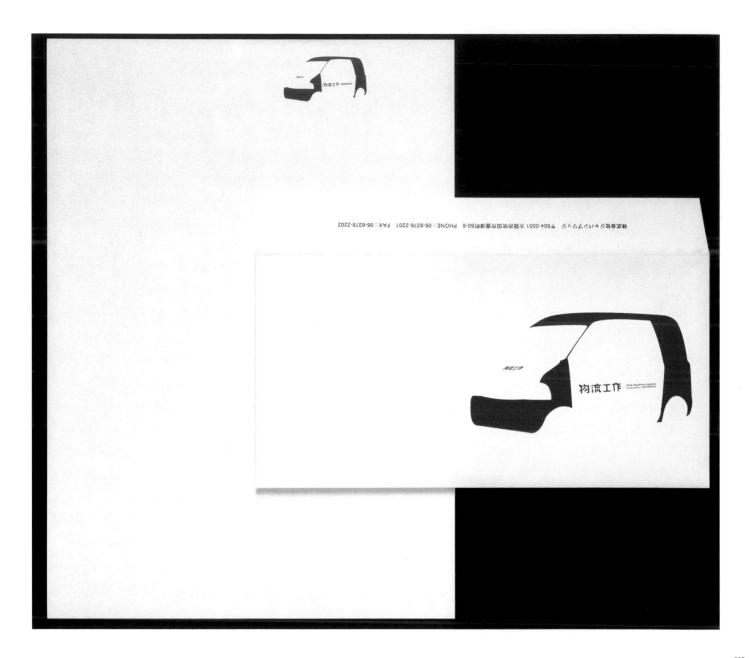

Television Commercial

Design_Kyle Cooper and Rafael Machó
Hollywood, California
Production_Lisa Laubhan
Editors_Jason Webb
and Lauren Giordano
Direction_Kyle Cooper
Agency Production_Robert Gondell
Art Director_Tom Rosenfield
Copywriter_Jeff Iorillo

Inferno Artist_Lori Freitag-Hild
2nd Animator_Rafael Machó
Coordination_Keith Bryant
and Chris Mantzaris

Agency_Foote, Cone & Belding
Design Office_Imaginary Forces
Client_Janus Mutual Funds

Principal Type_FF DIN (modified)

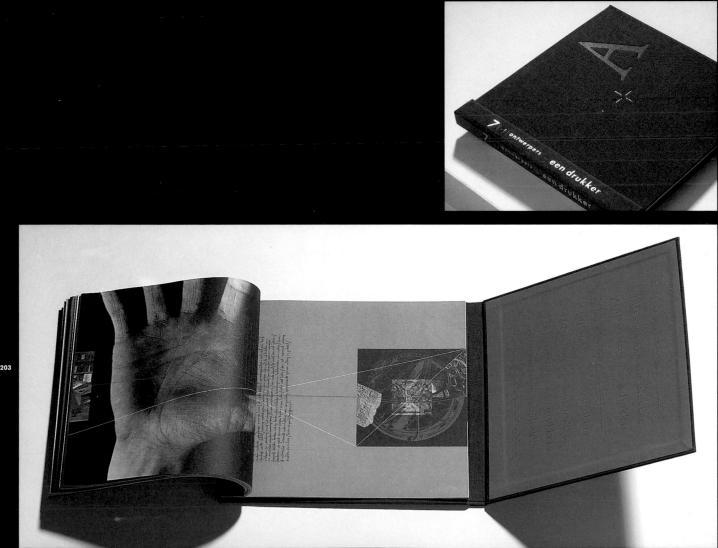

Book

Design_Hideki Nakajima
Tokyo, Japan
Lettering_Hideki Nakajima
Art Direction_Hideki Nakajima
Creative Direction_Hideki Nakajima
Photography_Various

Design Office_Nakajima Design
Client_CUT magazine/Rockin'on Inc.

Dimensions_8 7/16 x 11 5/16 in.
(21.5 x 30 cm)

Design_Karin Fong, Grant Lau,
and Chris Lopez
Hollywood, California
Producer_Anita Olan
Executive Producer_Saffron Kenny
Direction_Karin Fong
Creative Direction_Peter Frankfurt
Agency Producer_Kris Wong
Editor_Jeff Consiglio

Inferno Artist_Phil Man
and Danny Yoon
2D Animator_Jeff Jankens
Art Director_Bobby Appleby
Agency_Fallon McElliogott
Copywriter_Scott Vincent
Design Office_Imaginary Forces
Client_Qualcomm

Principal Type_T-26 Flux

100, 200 of zelfs

meer

dan 300

GOED

foto's voor

KOPE

tussen de

f400 en f100

(inderdaad, gratis

ENER

in de meeste gevallen

GIE

FontShop
heeft volgens
de laatste
schattingen
meer dan
100.000
foto's,
illustraties
en
achtergronden
in huis.

Foto's van
windmolens
bijvoorbeeld.
Van PhotoDisc,
John Foxx
(jawel, met
twee x en),
Digital Stock,
Goodshoot,
Stockbite,
Artville en zo
nog een paar
en indien
nodig heb je
ze morgen
allemaal in
huis. Voor
weinig, maar
voor
onbeperkt
gebruik.
Bel voor een
stuk of wat
starterkits
011-1-315 890,
of
e-mail naar
fontshop@
fontshop.be

Design_Uli Gürtler
Hamburg, Germany
Lettering_Uli Gürtler
Art Direction_Christina Petrich

Agency_Springer & Jacoby
Werbung GmbH
Client_Freie und Hansestadt
Hamburg

Principal Type_Handlettering

Design_Fons M. Hickmann
Berlin and Düsseldorf, Germany
Art Direction_Fons M. Hickmann
Editors_Siri Vorbeck,
Kristina Küompel, Nicole Koch,
and Stefan Lohmann
Publisher_Erwin Fey

Studio_Fons M. Hickmann
Client_zefa visual media

Principal Type_Corporate

Dimensions_11 ⁵⁄₁₆ x 18 ⅛ in.
(30 x 46 cm)

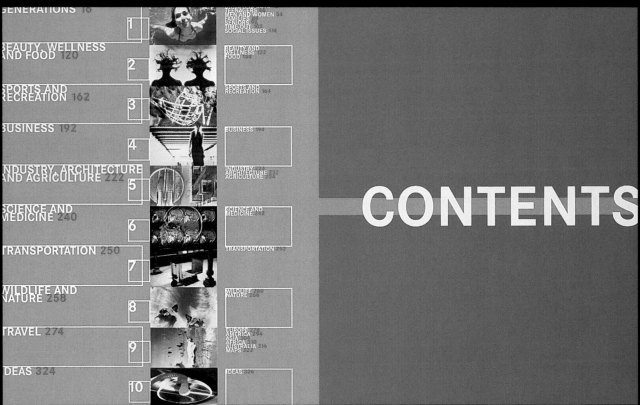

Design_Walter Bernard
and Mirko Ilić
New York, New York
Art Direction_Walter Bernard
and Mirko Ilić
Creative Direction_Walter Bernard
and Mirko Ilić

Design Office_WBMG, Inc.
and Mirko Ilić Design
Client_Neil Leifer

Principal Type_Bitstream Franklin
Gothic Condensed

Design_Len Cheeseman,
Hayden Doughty, Jason Bowden,
David Colquhoun, Tom Eslinger,
Brian Merrifield, and Tristam Sparks
Wellington, New Zealand
Art Direction_Len Cheeseman
Creative Direction_Gavin Bradley
Copywriters_Nigel Richardson
and Oliver Maisey
Producer_Tom Ackroyd

Agency_Saatchi & Saatchi
Wellington
Client_New Zealand Symphony
Orchestra

Principal Type_NZSO Non Regular

Design_Vanessa Marzaroli
Venice, California
Art Direction_Vanessa Marzaroli
Animator_Craig Tollifson
Producer_Casey Steele
Executive Producer_Matthew Marquis

Studio_Razorfish
Client_Travel Channel

Principal Type_Interstate
and Dot Mater Display

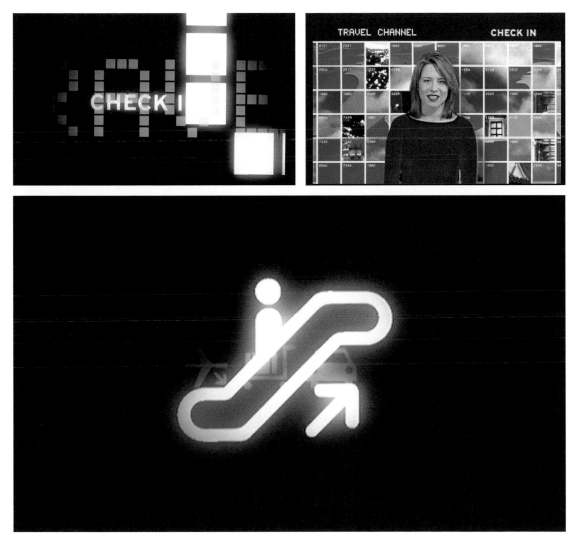

Design_Jun Takechi
Tokyo, Japan
Art Direction_Jun Takechi

Design Office_Jun Takechi
Client_Ruby in the Soda

Principal Type_Bank Gothic
Medium and Bolt Bold

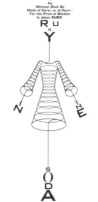

Design_Matt Eller
and Topher Sinkinson
Portland, Oregon
Art Direction_Matt Eller
Creative Direction_Alicia Johnson
Production Team_Sarah Starr,
Deborah Hyde, and Alan Foster
Creative Development_Alicia
Johnson, Amie Champagne,
Matt Eller, and Topher Sinkinson

Design Firm_Johnson & Wolverton
Client_Photonica USA

Principal Type_Univers   **Dimensions**_Various

215

Corporate Identity

Design_Teeranop Wangsillapakun
Chicago, Illinois
Lettering_Teeranop Wangsillapakun
Art Direction_Carlos Segura
Creative Direction_Carlos Segura

Studio_Segura Inc.
Client_yosho.com

Principal Type_Orator

Dimensions_Various

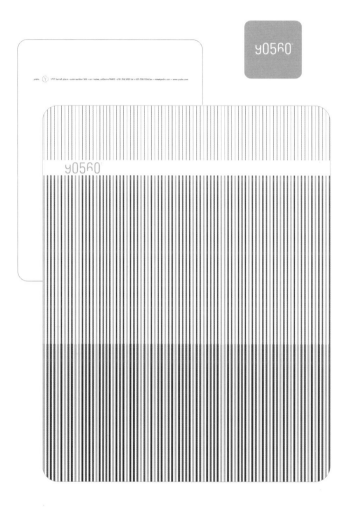

Design_Matt Checkowski
and Mikon van Gastel
Hollywood, California
Executive Producer_Saffron Kenny
and Dan Kolsrud
Producers_Alexander Dervin,
Chris Columbus, Mark Radcliffe,
and Michael Barnathan
Art Direction_Mikon van Gastel
Creative Direction_Peter Frankfurt
Editor_Jason Webb and
Nicholas DeToth

Inferno Artist_Nancy Hyland
2D Animators_Matt Checkowski
and Jennifer Lee
Coordinator_Christina Hwang
Distributor_Touchstone/Columbia
Pictures Entertainment
Post Production
Supervisor_Paula Dupre-Pesmen
Design Office_Imaginary Forces
Client_Chris Columbus

Principal Type_The Foundry Ballmer
ArchiType and the Foundry Gridnik

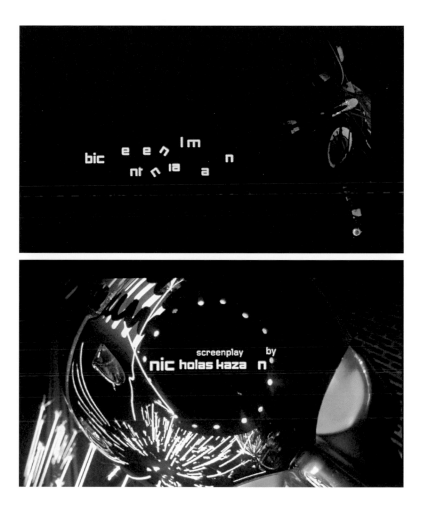

Design_Kirsten Dietz
Stuttgart, Germany
Art Direction_Kirsten Dietz
Creative Direction_Kirsten Dietz
and Jochen Rädeker

Agency_strichpunkt

Principal Type_FF TheSans

Dimensions_Various

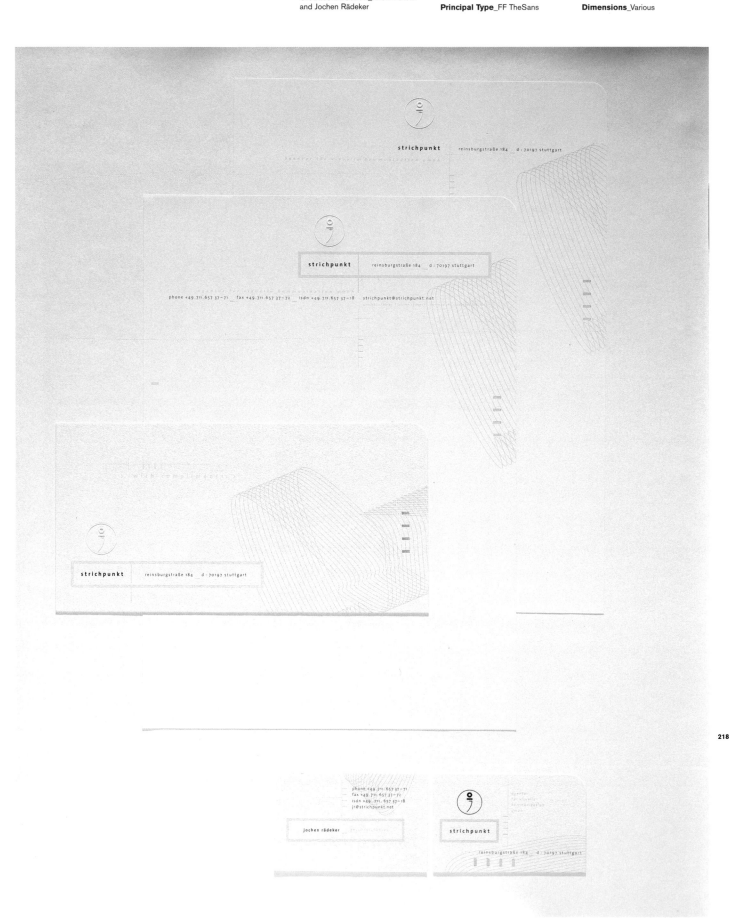

Design_Mirko Ilić
New York, New York
Art Direction_Mirko Ilić

Studio_Mirko Ilić Corp.
Client_Adam D. Tihany International,
Ltd., and the Time Hotel

Principal Type_Avenir

Dimensions_Various

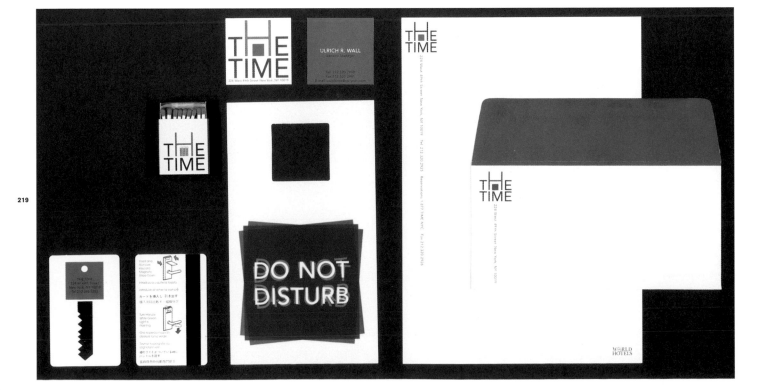

Design_ Mikon van Gastel
Hollywood, California
Coordinators_ Jono Golding
and Paul Madeira
3D Animators_ Sara Marandi
and Laurent Fauchere
Art Direction_ Kurt Mattila,
Mikon van Gastel, and Debra Pregler
Creative Direction_ John Parkinson
Executive Producer_ Bob Swensen
Producers_ Maureen Timpa,
Alexander Dervin, Denise Pouchet,
and Shelley Sink

Editor_ Kurt Mattila and Jeff Consiglio
Inferno Artist_ Danny Yoon and Phil Man
2D Animators_ Matt Cullen
and Matt Checkowski
Copywriter_ Jon Gustavson
Agency_DMB&B
Design Office_ Imaginary Forces
Client_ Cadillac EVOQ

Principal Type_FF DIN

Campaign

Design_Jens Gehlhaar
Los Angeles, California
Lettering_Jens Gehlhaar
Creative Direction_Seth Epstein

Design Office_Fuel

Principal Type_CIA Oddjob

Dimensions_Various

Design_ Joerg Bauer
Stuttgart, Germany
Art Direction_ Joerg Bauer
Creative Direction_ Uli Weber
and Joerg Bauer

Studio_ Joerg Bauer Design
Client_ Leonhardt + Kern
Werbung GmbH

Principal Type_ Filosofia,
Bell Gothic, and Trade Gothic

Dimensions_12 ³⁄₁₆ x 9 ¼ in.
(31 x 23.5 cm)

MICHAEL BILEK

Werbeagenturen ins
Handelsregister
eintragen, das
können alle. Eine
Werbeagentur als
Geldmaschine
betreiben, das tun
viele. Eine
Werbeagentur zum
Markenzeichen
machen, das gelingt
w e n i g e n.

R e s p e k t !

Book

Design_Silja Götz, Floridan Koch,
Rafael Koch, Peter Körner,
Urs Lehni, and Marcus Wohlhüter
Hamburg, Germany, London,
England, and Lucerne, Switzerland
Art Direction_Katja Fössel,
Ralf Herms, and Maurizio Poletto
Creative Direction_Ralf Herms
Photography_Johannes Paffrath,
Iris Döring, and Konstanze Wagenhofer

Studio_+rosebud

Principal Type_Adobe Garamond
and HTF Champion Gothic

Dimensions_7 ½ x 11 ⁷⁄₁₆ in.
(19 x 29.7 cm)

Teaser Trailer

Design_Matt Cullen
Hollywood, California
Executive Producer_Bob Swensen
Direction_Kurt Mattila
and Luc Besson
Live Action
Producer_Denise Pouchet
Creative Direction_Peter Frankfurt
Post Production
Producer_Anita Olan

Coordinator_Seri Bryant
Editors_Kurt Mattila
and Mark Hoffman
Inferno Artist_Phil Man
2D Animator_Matt Cullen
Director of Photography_Vilmos
Zsigmond, ASC
Producer_Patrice Ledoux
Copywriter_Tucker Parsons

Design Office_Imaginary Forces
Client_Columbia TriStar

Principal Type_Caslon Antique

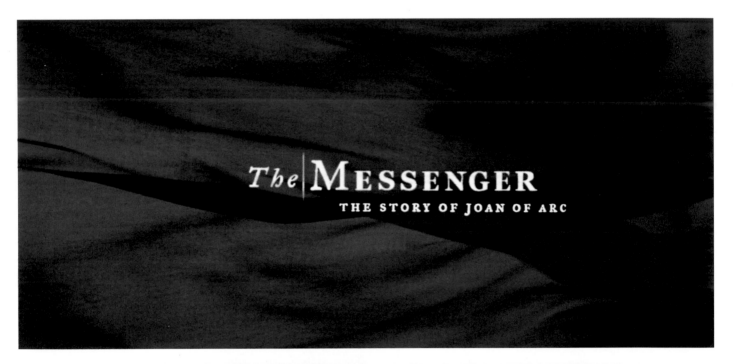

Design_Kyle Cooper,
Eric Cruz and Mike Jakab
Hollywood, California
Executive Producer_Saffron Kenny
and Kevin Jarre
Producers_Alexander Dervin,
James Jacks, and Sean Daniel
Art Direction_Kyle Cooper
Direction_Stephen Sommers
Editors_Lauren Giordano
and Bob Ducsay

Inferno Artist_Danny Yoon
and Elton Garcia
**Post Production
Supervisor**_Doreen Dixon
2D Animator_Ben Lopez
3D Animators_Emily Goodman
and Jim Goodman
Coordinator_Jono Golding
Design Office_Imaginary Forces
Client_Universal

Principal Type_La Mummia

Design_Rymn Massand
New York, New York
Creative Direction_Michael Ian Kaye
Photography_Daniel Bibb

Studio_Little, Brown and Company

Principal Type_Univers Condensed   **Dimensions**_6 x 9¼ in.
(15.2 x 23.5 cm)

Design_Gijs Sierman
Amsterdam, The Netherlands
Art Direction_van Lindonk Special
Projects and Gijs Sierman
Creative Direction_van Lindonk
Special Projects
Concept_Peter van Lindonk

Agency_van Lindoink
Special Projects
Studio_Gijs Sierman
Client_Albert Heijn

Principal Type_ITC Century
and Trade Gothic

Dimensions_10 ⅞₆ x 9 ⅞ in.
(26 x 25 cm)

Book

Design_Johannes Erler
and Manus Fahrner
Hamburg, Germany
Art Direction_Johannes Erler
Creative Direction_Johannes Erler
Photography_Heribert Schindler
and Ulrich Hoppe
Text_Jan Weiler

Design Office_Factor Design
Client_Römerturm Feinpapiere

Principal Type_Monotype Van
Dijck, Univers, Akzidenz Grotesk,
and Emigre Ten

Dimensions_9 ¼ x 12 ³⁄₁₆ in.
(23.5 x 31 cm)

Student Work

Design_Oliver Henn
Düsseldorf, Germany

School_Fachhochschule
Düsseldorf
Instructors_Jean Ulysses Voelker
and Professor Roland Henss

Principal Type_Bell Gothic   **Dimensions**_8 ³⁄₁₆ x 7 in.
(20.8 x 17.8 cm)

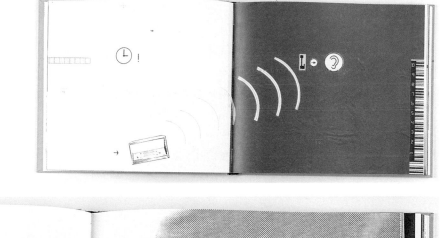

231

Book

Design_Various Students
Pasadena, California
Art Direction_Vance Studley
Creative Direction_Vance Studley

School_Archetype Press at
Art Center College of Design
Client_Art Center College of Design

Principal Type_Various foundry types

Dimensions_8 x 12 in.
(20.3 x 30.5 cm)

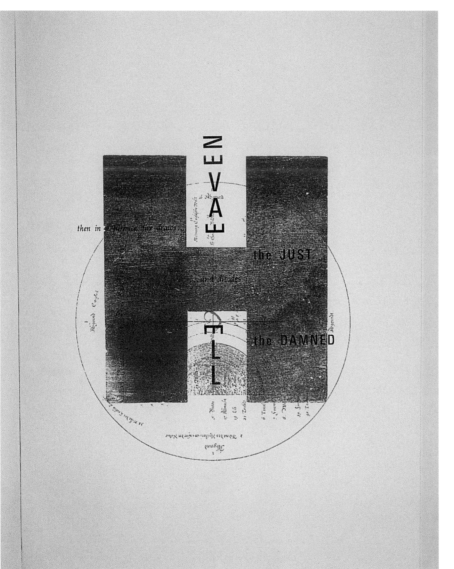

Design_David Shields
and Mark Todd
San Marcos, Texas

Studio_White Gas

Principal Type_ITC Franklin Gothic

Dimensions_9½ x 7 in.
(24.1 x 17.8 cm)

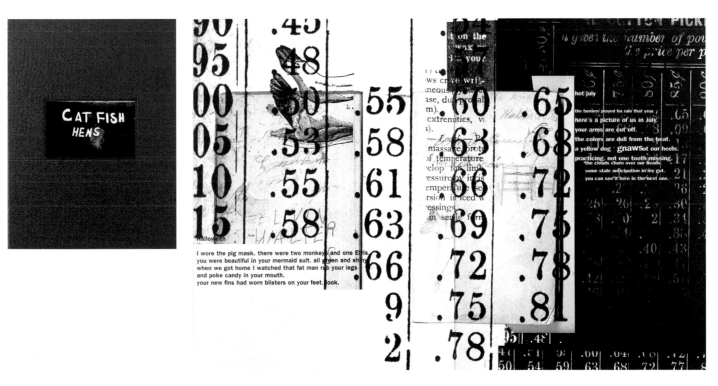

Television Commercial

Design_Christopher Wargin
Santa Monica, California
Art Direction_Gordon Melcher
Creative Direction_Christopher
Wargin and Larry Kopald

Agency_Think New Ideas
Design Office_PRoGRESS
bureau of design
Client_Oracle

Principal Type_Bawdy

Design_Michael Bierut
and Kerrie Powell
New York, New York
Art Direction_Michael Bierut

Design Office_Pentagram
Client_Yale School of Architecture

Principal Type_ITC Franklin Gothic
and various

Dimensions_12 ½ x 9 in.
(31.8 x 22.9 cm)

235

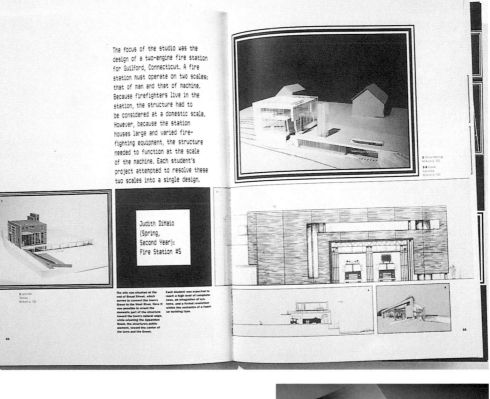

Design_Helmut Himmler
and Judith Treder
Frankfurt, Germany
Lettering_Judith Treder
Art Direction_Helmut Himmler
Creative Direction_Rolf Greulich
Copywriter_Dirk Galia

Agency_Michael Conrad
& Leo Burnett

Principal Type_Rechtmann Script,
ITC Franklin Gothic Compressed,
and Confidential

Dimensions_6 ⅞ x 9 ⁷⁄₁₆ in.
(17.5 x 24 cm)

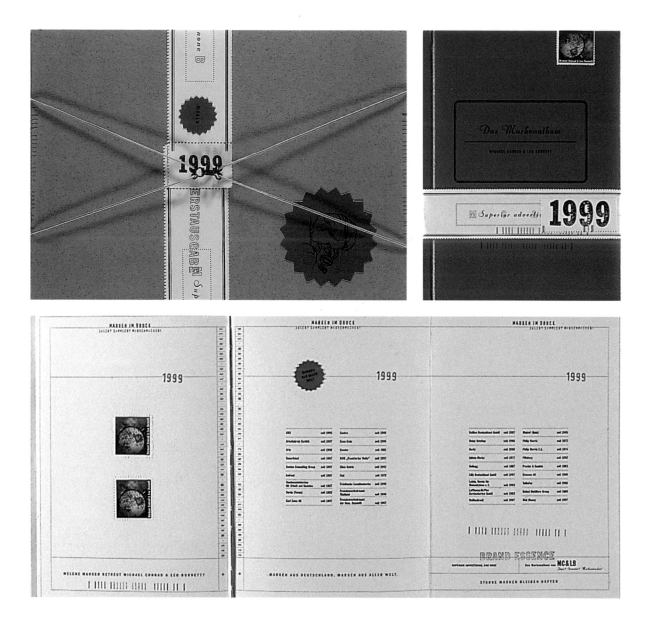

Book

Design_Stefan Sagmeister
New York, New York
Art Direction_Stefan Sagmeister
and David Byrne
Creative Direction_Stefan
Sagmeister and David Byrne
Photography_David Byrne

Design Office_Sagmeister Inc.
Client_David Byrne

Principal Type_Trade Gothic,
Helvetica, Frutiger, and handlettering

Dimensions_11 x 14 in.
(27.9 x 35.6 cm)

Design_Camille Utterback
and Romy Achituv
New York, New York

School_Interactive
Telecommunciations Program/
New York University

Principal Type_Windows OS
System Fixed font

Design_David Shrimpf
Minneapolis, Minnesota
Creative Direction_Bill Thorburn
Photography_Chuck Smith
Copywriter_Chuck Smith

Design Office_Carmichael
Lynch Thorburn
Client_Poof

Principal Type_V.A.G Rounded

Dimensions_8 ½ x 11 in.
(21.6 x 27.9 cm)

Design_Victor Corpuz
Malibu, California
Art Direction_Jane Kobayashi

Design Office_5D Studio
Client_16 X 16 Visual User
Interface Design

Principal Type_Microscan

Dimensions_8 ½ x 11 in.
(21.6 x 27.9 cm)

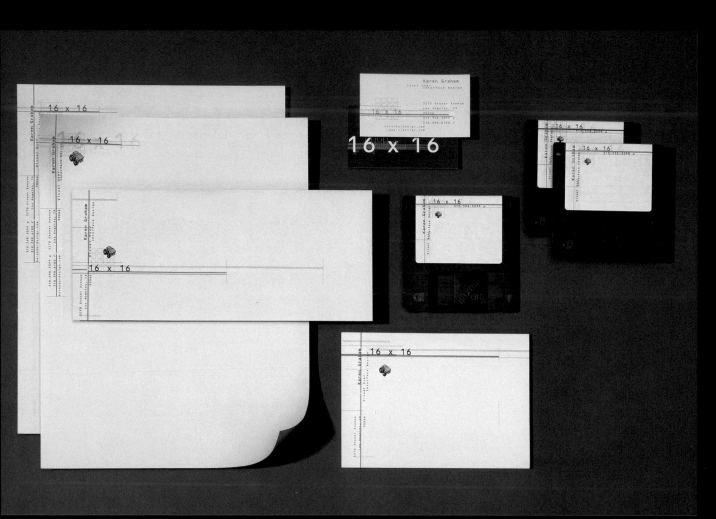

Design_Douglas Dearden
Salt Lake City, Utah
Lettering_Douglas Dearden
and Dan Longhuest
Art Direction_Douglas Dearden

Design Office_AND

Principal Type_Adobe Garamond

Dimensions_8 ½ x 11 in.
(21.6 x 27.9 cm)

Magazine

Design_J. Abbott Miller,
Scott Devendorf, and Roy Brooks
New York, New York
Art Direction_J. Abbott Miller

Design Office_Pentagram
Client_2wice Arts Foundation

Principal Type_FF Scala Sans

Dimensions_11½ x 8¼ in.
(29.2 x 21 cm)

243

Poster

Design_Hiroaki Nagai
and Hiroaki Seki
Tokyo, Japan
Art Direction_Hiroaki Nagai
Creative Direction_Kenichi Aki
Photography_Kazumi Kurigami
Copywriter_Masakazu Nifuji

Agency_Yomiko Advertising Inc.
Studio_N • G., Inc.
Client_Onward Kashiyama Co., Ltd.

Principal Type_Gothic MB101

Dimensions_57 ⁵⁄₁₆ x 40 ⁹⁄₁₆ in.
(145.6 x 103 cm)

Poster

Design_Philippe Apeloig
Paris, France
Art Direction_Philippe Apeloig

Agency_Apeloig Design
Client_Cité du Livre, Aix-en-Provence

Principal Type_Univers Extra Black

Dimensions_47 ¼ x 67 ¾ in.
(120 x 172 cm)

245

Design_Brode Vosloo
Durban, South Africa
Lettering_Brode Vosloo
Art Direction_Brode Vosloo

Creative Direction_Brode Vosloo
Agency_Orange Juice Design (Pty) Ltd.
Client_Pro Helvetica,
Art Council of Switzerland

Principal Type_Various

Dimensions_16 ⁹⁄₁₆ x 11 ⁷⁄₁₆ in.
(42 x 29.7 cm)

Design_Matthew Beckerle
Toronto, Canada
Creative Direction_Matthew
Beckerle
Photography_Tim Morrison

Studio_Creative Activity
Design Company
Client_Blonde Magazine

Principal Type_Melior
and Univers Condensed

Dimensions_8 ⅜ x 11 in.
(21.3 x 27.9 cm)

Poster

Design_Katsunori Nishi
Tokyo, Japan
Art Direction_Katsunori Nishi

Design Office_Brahman
company limited

Principal Type_Worm Hole

Dimensions_40 ⅝ x 28 ⅝ in.
(103 x 72.8 cm)

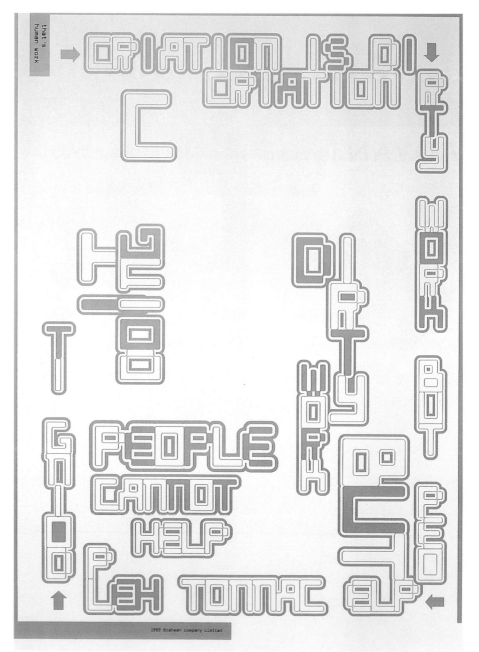

Book

Design_Susana Rodriguez,
Hans Seeger, and Dave Ritter
Chicago, Illinois
Creative Direction_Curtis Schreiber
Editor_Mike Wang and Fred Guterl

Agency_VSA Partners
Client_IBM

Principal Type_Interstate

Dimensions_11 x 15 in.
(27.9 x 38.1 cm)

253

Book Cover

Design_ Benjamin Pham
San Francisco, California
Art Direction_ Patricia Evangelista
Photography_ Makota Kubota

Studio_ Character
Client_ Chronicle Books

Principal Type_ Gill Sans
and Futura BT Medium, and
Futura BT Bold

Dimensions_10 ¹⁄₁₆ x 13 ½ in.
(25.6 x 34.3 cm)

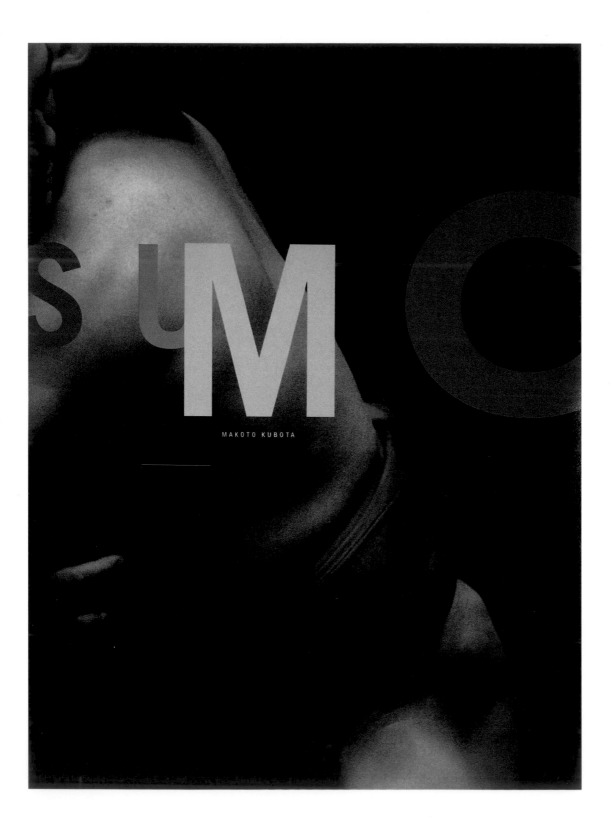

Magazine

Design_Domenic Lippa
and Richard McGillan
Twickenham, England
Art Direction_Domenic Lippa
Creative Direction_Domenic Lippa
Editor_Patrick Baglee
Assistant Editor_Clare Lundy

Studio_Lippa Pearce Design
Client_Typographic Circle

Principal Type_Zurich

Dimensions_11 x 14 in.
(28 x 35.5 cm)

Design_Bill Douglas
Toronto, Canada

Studio_The Bang
Client_Coupe

Principal Type_Trade Gothic,
Times New Roman, and Helvetica

Dimensions_9 ⅝ x 11 ½ in.
(24.5 x 29. 2 cm)

Design_Guy Pask,
Aaron O'Donnel,
and Alec Bathgate
Christchurch, New Zealand
Art Direction_Guy Pask
Creative Direction_Guy Pask
and Douglas Maclean

Design Office_Strategy
Advertising & Design
Client_Robert McDougall
Art Gallery

Principal Type_Adobe Jenson
and Monotype Grotesque

Dimensions_11 ¹¹⁄₁₆ x 8 ¼ in.
(29.7 x 21 cm)

Magazine Spread

Design_Bill Douglas
Toronto, Canada
Photography_Glenda Stuart

Studio_The Bang
Client_Coupe

Principal Type_Trade Gothic

Dimensions_19 ¼ x 11 ½ in.
(24.5 x 29.2 cm)

Magazine Spread

Design_Frank Gehrke
Munich, Germany
Art Direction_Horst Moser

Studio_Independent Medien – Design
Client_Computerwoche – Verlag I.D.G.

Principal Type_ITC Officina Sans

Dimensions_21⁷⁄₁₆ x 15 in.
(54.5 x 38 cm)

Visionen

TITEL

Hinterbliebene nach Suizid

Der doppelte Tod

Tod

Wenn er dem Leben mit uns den Tod vorgezogen hat: Wie soll mich auf der Welt irgendjemand sonst wertschätzen?

261

Beverley war eine Powerfrau, engagiert und kontaktfreudig. Ganze Gesellschaften konnte sie zum Lachen bringen, wenn sie den Clown spielte. „Niemand hatte so etwas mit ihr in Verbindung gebracht", sagt ihre damalige Lebensgefährten Chris Paul. Sie hatte die 26-Jährige nach ihrem zweiten Suizidversuch kennengelernt und musste nach zweieinhalb Jahren miteinander geteilten Lebens die „fürchterliche Erfahrung" machen, dass „Liebe kein Allheilmittel ist". Als abends spät ein Polizist an ihrer Tür klingelte, wusste Chris schon Bescheid. „In ihrem Keller hängt eine junge Frau", sagte er, einfühlsam wie ein Stadtwerker, der zum Stromableser kommt. Ein polizeiliches Rollkommando fegte durch die Wohnung, beschlagnahmte Beverleys Kalender und ein Gedicht, das über ihrem Schreibtisch hing. Als Chris sich weigerte, die Leiche zu identifizieren, wurden die Polizisten wütend. „Der Sanitäter, der sie abhol-

te, war der Einzige, der mal danach fragte, wie es mir geht." Beverleys Körper wurde abtransportiert in die gerichtliche Kühlkammer. Es war Freitagabend. Übers Wochenende waren dort keine Dienststellen. „Bei ihrem Körper zu sein", erinnert sich die überlebende Gefährten, „hatte sehr geholfen."

Ende der Normalität

1997 setzten in Deutschland 12.201 Menschen ihrem Leben selbst ein Ende. Zurück bleiben schätzungsweise 400000 Jassungslose Angehörige: Lebenspartner, Kinder, Mütter, Väter, Geschwister, Großeltern, Freunde. Sie erleben den Verlust ihrer Angehörigen, wie eine zurückgelassene Ehefrau formuliert, als einen „doppelten Tod". Denn sie haben nicht nur die Trauer zu bewältigen, sondern auch die Scham und die Schuldgefühle für dieses Ende. Denn Suizid ist kein „normaler" Tod.

„Es ist, als ob ich mit einem Kains-

mahl behaftet bin", klagt eine junge Frau aus Karlsruhe. Vor acht Monaten wurde sie mit ihren beiden acht und zehn Jahre alten Kindern allein im Leben zurückgelassen. „Ich konnte nicht einmal mehr mit aufrechten Gang den Müll wegbringen." Den Satz: „Mein Mann hat sich das Leben genommen" hat sie erst mühsam aussprechen lernen müssen. Als ein Versicherungsvertreter bei ihr anrief, gab sie spontan die falsche Auskunft, ihr Mann sei bei einem Unfall gestorben.

Dabei gab es den Suizid zu allen Zeiten und in allen Gesellschaften. Dennoch tragen sich die Zurückgelassenen: „Was haben wir falsch gemacht?" Als ob ein Mensch einen anderen retten könnte, wenn der es selber gar nicht will. „Wir mussten dem anderen auch die Würde und Verantwortung für sein Leben lassen", beschreibt Chris Paul die Gratwanderung der Freunde und Angehörigen suizidgefährdeter Menschen. „Wir können doch nicht alle

Freunde, die in eine Krise geraten, in die Psychiatrie einweisen lassen." Manchmal passiert die Katastrophe nach langen Depressionen, manchmal wie aus heiterem Himmel. Barbara Sillack wurde, nach 25-jährigem Zusammenleben, plötzlich von ihrem Mann verlassen. „Waren unsere neunzährige Tochter und ich ihm nichts wert gewesen?", fragt sie verzweifelt. Das nagt am Selbstwertgefühl. „Wenn schon mein Mann den Tod einem Leben mit mir vorgezogen hatte, wie sollte dann irgendjemand sonst auf der Welt mich wertschätzen?" Sie fühlt sich nicht nur um die gemeinsame Zukunft betrogen, sondern auch um die Vergangenheit. War sie gar nicht so glücklich gewesen, wie sie es erlebt hatte?

„Angehörige von Suizidtoten", weiß Ellen Wittke, Sprecherin der Arbeitskreise Leben in Baden-Württemberg (AKL), „sind selbst in hohem Maß suizidgefährdet. Sie gelten als ausgewiesene Risikogruppe." In diesem Jahr fand die bundesweit erste

Tagung für Trauernde nach einem Suizid und ihre Helfer(innen) – die häufig selbst Betroffene sind – statt. Betroffene aus ganz Deutschland und der Schweiz waren gekommen, um „Menschen zu treffen, die das Gleiche erlebt haben wie ich".

Trauer nach Suizid ist anders

Trauergruppen, die dem Tod seine soziale Dimension wieder abgewinnen wollen, gibt es schon viele in Deutschland. Trauernde nach einem Suizid fühlen sich in diesen Gruppen nicht aufgehoben. Sie bleiben meist isoliert mit ihrer Trauer, Schuld und Scham. Eine Tochter, deren Mutter im Januar in den Tod gegangen ist, hat die Teilnahme an der Tagung ihrem Vater zum Geburtstag geschenkt. „Zu Hause habe ich niemanden kennengelernt, der so etwas aus eigener Erfahrung kennt." Er ist der einzige Mann in einer Runde von etwa 20 Betroffenen. Das spiegelt die Statistik. Zu zwei Dritteln sind es Män-

ner, die sich das Leben nehmen. In der Gruppe kommen Frauen zusammen, die ihre Männer oder Söhne verloren. Einige haben beide Eltern und weitere Familienangehörige durch Suizid verloren.

Eine Frau aus Nordrhein-Westfalen musste vor zwölf Jahren den plötzlichen Herztod ihres Ehemannes hinnehmen. Nun hat sich ihr neuer Partner das Leben genommen. Nach drei Wochen ließen sich die meisten Freunde nicht mehr blicken. „Es wurde totgeschwiegen, als hätte es die sechs Jahre mit ihm nie gegeben. Das tut weh." Von ihrer Umgebung

LITERATUR

Chris Paul
Warum hast du uns das angetan?
Ein Begleitbuch für Trauernde, wenn sich jemand das Leben genommen hat.
Gütersloh 1998, 24,80 DM

TRAUER SCHULD UND

Indice

2

3 Avvertenze per il pubblico 4 Calendario degli spettacoli per gli abbonati 21 XL Stagione Concertistica 38 Abbonamenti e biglietti 40 Il Teatro Rossini 6 21/22/23/24 ottobre 1999 **NATALE IN CASA CUPIELLO** di Eduardo De Filippo 10 4/5/6/7 novembre 1999 **IL MALATO IMMAGINARIO** di Molière 14 25/26/27/28/29 novembre 1999 **AMLETO** di William Shakespeare 18 10/11/12 dicembre 1999 **SCENE D'AMOR PERDUTO** da William Shakespeare di Massimo Navone e Giampiero Solari 22 13/14/15/16 gennaio 2000 **PENSACI, GIACOMINO!** di Luigi Pirandello 26 10/11/12/13 febbraio 2000 **IL RINOCERONTE** di Eugène Ionesco 30 24/25/26/27 febbraio 2000 **HEDDA GABLER** di Henrik Ibsen 34 6/7/8/9 aprile 2000 **NOVECENTO** di Alessandro Baricco

Avvertenze per il pubblico

Gli abbonati sono tenuti a rispettare date e turni di abbonamento secondo il calendario pubblicato a pagina 4/5 del presente libretto. Si precisa che durante la stagione non sarà in alcun caso possibile cambiare turno. Non è previsto alcun rimborso per gli spettacoli non fruiti. Gli abbonamenti non sono nominativi e possono essere ceduti ad altre persone; quelli a tariffa ridotta possono essere ceduti solo a persone aventi diritto alla medesima agevolazione. Lo spettatore deve essere sempre munito di biglietto, tessera d'abbonamento o d'ingresso, da esibire al personale di sala addetto al controllo su semplice richiesta. Nel corso delle rappresentazioni, ad eccezione di specifiche autorizzazioni della Direzione del Teatro e della Compagnia ospitata, è vietato l'uso di apparecchi fotografici o di registrazione audio e video. Gli spettatori sono pregati di spegnere i telefoni cellulari prima di entrare in Teatro. Attenzione: le date degli spettacoli possono subire variazioni per cause di forza maggiore. Si raccomanda agli spettatori di verificare le date degli stessi sul materiale informativo (locandine e manifesti) che viene esposto in Teatro, e di prestare attenzione a eventuali annunci dello speaker. In caso di annullamento dello spettacolo il relativo biglietto verrà rimborsato nei giorni successivi. Qualora non fosse possibile il recupero o la sostituzione dello spettacolo annullato, verranno rimborsate anche le rispettive quote agli abbonati. Salvo diversa indicazione gli spettacoli avranno inizio alle ore 21.00 nei giorni feriali e alle ore 17.00 la domenica e i giorni festivi.

Si raccomanda la massima puntualità, a spettacolo iniziato è vietato l'accesso alla platea e ai posti numerati di galleria.

Design_Bill Douglas
Toronto, Canada
Photography_Johnny Chavez

Studio_The Bang

Principal Type_Times New Roman

Dimensions_19 ¼ x 1
(24.5 x 29.2 cm)

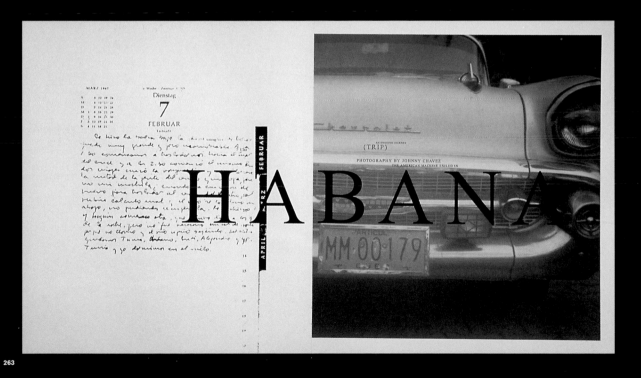

Design_Iwao Miura, Rikiya Tanaka, and Mizuho Hayashi
Tokyo, Japan
Art Direction_Iwao Miura
Creative Direction_Atsushi Shikano
Editor-in-Chief_Atsushi Shikano
Editors_Shinji Hyogo
and Koremasa Uno

Studio_rockin'on inc.
design department
Client_rockin'on, Buzz Magazine

Dimensions_10 ¼ x 16 ⁹⁄₁₆ in.
(26 x 42 cm)

Poster

Design_Leonardo Sonnoli,
Rimini, Italy
Art Direction_Leonardo Sonnoli

Studio_Dolcini Associati

Principal Type_Walker and Bell
Centennial

Dimensions_27 ⁹⁄₁₆ x 39 ⅜ in.
(70 x 100 cm)

© Sergio Polano 1999

267

Lecturer	→ MATTHEW CARTER	City	→ PESARO>ITALY
Date	→ 24-04-1999	Design	→ LEONARDO SONNOLI
Place	→ DOLCINI ASSOCIATI	Type	→ WALKER + BELL CENTENNIAL

TypeDirectorsClub
TDC² 2000

TDC 46+ P.271

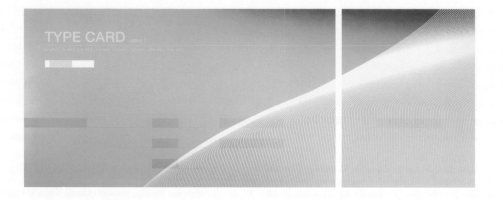

SECTION CONTAINS: 4 Judges Biographies and Sample Work.
Judges: Matthew Carter Barry Deck John Hudson Kathleen Tinkel

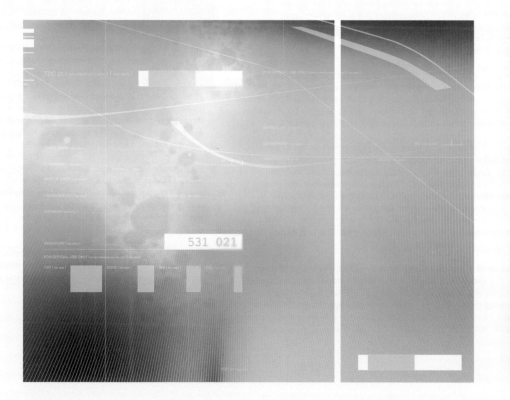

531 021

+

TypeDirectorsClub
TDC² 2000 The Judges

TDC 46+ P.274

J.01   Matthew Carter
J.02   Barry Deck

TypeDirectorsClub
TDC² 2000 Judges' Work

TDC 46+ P.278

MATTHEW·CARER'S
MANTINIA
A·NEW·DESIGN
WITH·CAPITALs
TALL·CAPITALS
ALERNATIVES
SUPERIORS·&
LIGATURES

279

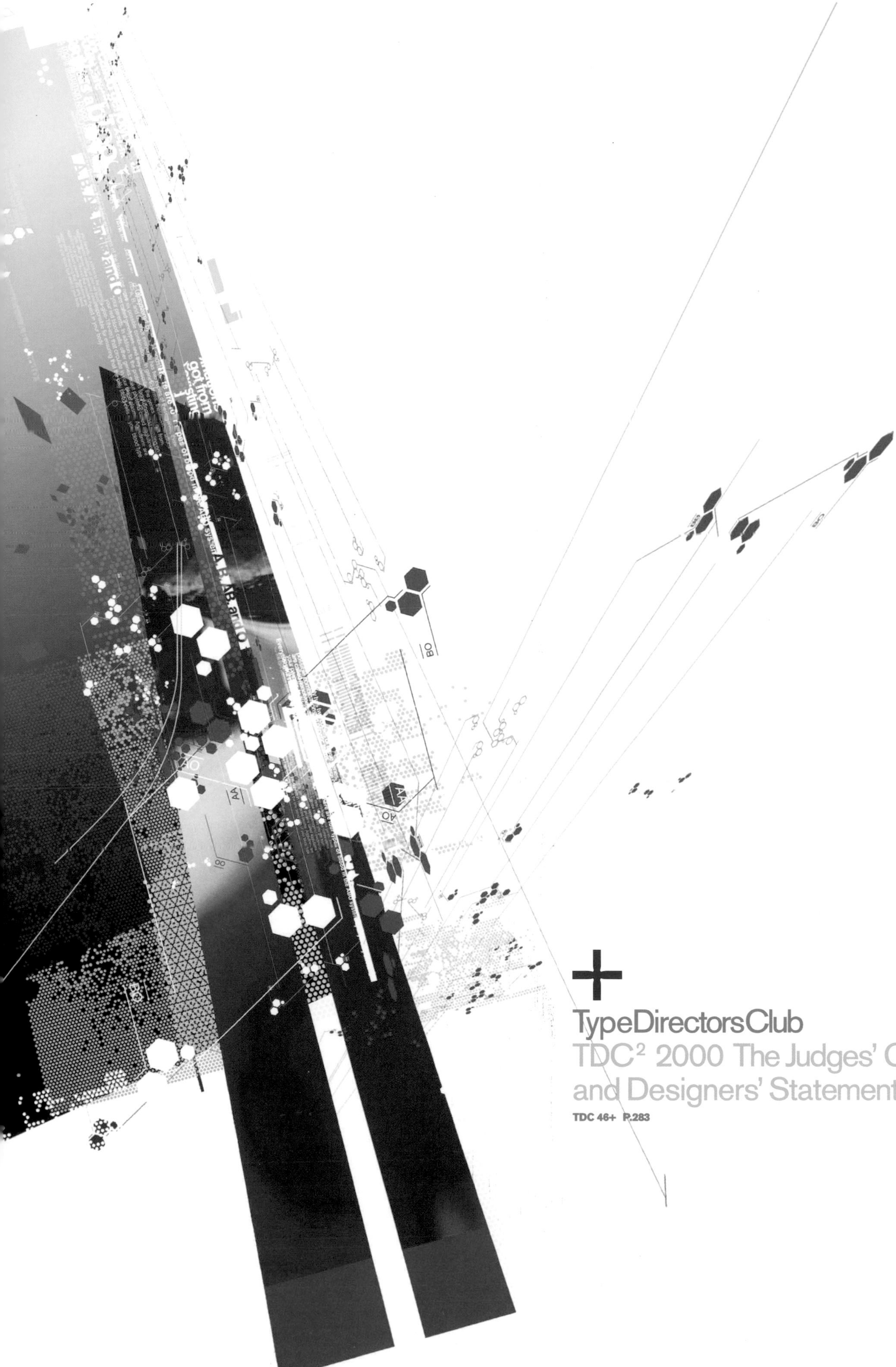

+

TypeDirectorsClub
TDC² 2000 The Judges' Choices
and Designers' Statements
TDC 46+   P.283

Biblon

Design_František Štorm,
Czech Republic

Type Foundry_Štorm Type Foundry

Family_Regular, Bold: Roman,
Italic (each in Normal and SC
character sets)

J.01   Matthew Carter

D.01.5 František Štorm

ABCDEFGHIJKLMNOPQ RSTUVWXYZ1234567890
ABCDEFGHIJKLMNOPQRSTUVWXYZ
abcdefghijklmnopqrstuvwxyz 1234567890

Two terms, Baroque and Rococo, are used by František Štorm in his description of Biblon, and perhaps both are needed to do justice to its sheer exuberance. Hardly a period piece, this splendid typeface, but somewhere in it a historical style is either waving or drowning. There may be a clue in the text used to show the face to the TDC jury, in archaic French complete with long esses, taken from the 1621 specimen of Jean Jannon, that impertinent and ever-so-slightly cack-handed invigorator of Garamond's stately legacy. Wherever František Štorm got his inspiration, he took nothing for granted. No convention is safe: the Roman and Italic are condensed; the small caps are wider (they are also smaller than the lowercase, while they're at it, and float nonchalantly above the baseline in the Italic). Horizontal serifs in the Roman lowercase, where they exist at all, are turned inward to give the letterforms a pigeon-toed stance that adds to the general jauntiness. No two strokes in the Italic are in parallel, whence its syncopated rhythm—and its legibility. A couple of the swashest Italic capitals have gone over the top in the direction of whimsy, but this seems a small price to pay for the overall vigor of this wonderfully uninhibited design. Great stuff.

In our modern times people print ever more futile ideas and intersperse them with many blank pages. There is no need to economize on paper and to look out for optically narrowed type faces. An opposite situation is in every biblical society where the editors must cram a text containing some 2000 pages into a single volume. That is where there is a need for type faces which are economizing, legible and spiritually cultivated. The new Biblon type face, therefore, does not need to rely on a wide range of sizes; it is sufficient if it looks well from approximately five to eighteen points. Its elegance decreases commensurately with its increasing size. In poster sizes the speculative construction of the letter form is already revealed—the points of gravity of the strokes are shifted as much as possible in the horizontal directions and the crotches—the spaces between the rounded stroke and the shaft—are emphasized. In small-size letters we hardly notice that almost all horizontal serifs (if they have not disappeared entirely) have been pushed inside the letter form so that they should not hamper the adjacent letters. To quieten the lines, the accents have been miniaturized as well. The figures have uniform width and avow the lower case principle. The italics of Biblon have been stylized more daringly, with the use of long-forsaken Rococo elements. The slanted designs of the small capitals have upper case letters slightly submerged under the capital line, in order to enhance the decorative character of titles and headings. Biblon has a large x-height of lower-case letters and one can get used to its compressed proportions. Many condensed type faces leave a feeling of distress after longer reading. Here, however, this has been sophisticatedly eliminated. We have availed ourselves in this type face design also of several optical tricks dating from fairly recent period, but our main source of inspiration was the daringness of type designers of the 18th century. Underneath the contemporary-looking design of Biblon one can conjecture a Baroque play with the shifting of shadows, intentional overstatement or absolute simplification of forms. Even though Biblon probably will not be used for its purpose in the near future, it represents a very sound body type.

Summa Gambit

Design_Damir Gamulin,
Zagreb, Croatia

Family_Regular

J.02 Barry Deck

D.02.5 Damir Gamulin

beton three

100% concrete

.abcdefghijklmnopqrstuvwxyz
.ABCDEFGHIJKLMNOPQRSTUVWXYZ
.0123456789.,:!"≠$%&'[ø]=?+/+-
.{‡}≤±≥¶ bonez @<µΔ≠¢∑>∏¯ß ø ® © ‰

I enjoyed the references to chain-link fencing, coat hangers, OCR computer type and the automatic smoothing function of early bitmap fonts. It reminds me of what I got when I printed Geneva from MacDraw in 1987. Sort of like a pseudo-futuristic version of Zuzana Licko's Citizen with these eastern block gulag references thrown in. But, I really chose it because I want the designer to work on it some more. I would like to see some of these bent wire references articulated more solidly. Some of the shapes seem a little tentative to me; the stem on the h, for instance. They're not deliberately curved, nor geometric, neither here nor there. The broken characters don't work for me. This move seems unrelated to the other ideas in the face. I enjoy the shapes in the o, six, seven, nine, dollar sign, percent sign and ampersand, characters which come closest to what the face should be.

Working on Summa Gambit I had light, architectonic aesthetics in mind. I wanted to reveal joints that would normally stay hidden under the 'bold' cover. As a result you get an 'imperfect' font. Summa is first in the line of the typefaces created using a single principle—accumulating details on uniform centerlines that serve as basic construction elements. And yes, it also reflects my desire to lose weight.

287

Chêneau/Lyons

Design_Daniel Carr, USA

Type Foundry_Golgonooza Letter
Foundry & Press

Family_Roman (Chêneau),
Italic (Lyons)

J.04   Kathleen Tinkel

D.04.5   Daniel Carr

Name

Chêneau

Roman, *Italic* & Small Capitals
with *Lyons Italic*

To be vital and permanent a work of art (it seems to me) must, to begin with, bear evidence that its author possessed each of three things, intellect, passion, and skill. Intellect and skill, without passion, give us only cold academicism; passion and skill, without intellect, fail to appeal to our intelligence; intellect and passion without skill, are inarticulate. In a work of art we must therefore look for these qualities, the absence of any one which means that a painting or a piece of sculpture is merely a futile exercise. This is only a primary test, but it is to this test that works of art must first of all be put, in order that their primary significance may be measured. Who among painters and sculptors, past and present, will, in *your opinion,* pass this test? That is the question.

Porter Garnett
What is it?
An Aesthetical Investigation

With Chêneau and Lyons display italic, type designer Dan Carr does an interesting job of exploiting digital technology to simulate letterforms of hundreds of years ago. But the result is a hybrid that fails both as a museum piece and as a useful digital font for today. Photo-offset printing can never replicate the look and feel of 16th-century pages. We miss the subtle 3D effect and subtle shadowing of pages printed in relief, and are compelled to notice the contrived irregularities of the digital font for what they are.

Like many other fonts based on designs of the past, Chêneau also suffers from lack of what is arguably the most important technique used for ancient typefaces, a separate design for each size. Instead of trying to recreate the past, I'd echo the concerns of type designers Hermann Zapf, Warren Chappell, and others when they ask not only whether we can faithfully simulate ancient typefaces, but should we even try.

Chêneau Roman, Italic and Small Capitals with Lyons Italic is a small type family with a display italic font included, they are my first digital typefaces. Simultaneously I cut a metal typeface called Regulus using traditional hand punchcutting. My purpose for both was the same; I wanted to have typefaces in both mediums that would express visible forms of my voice as a writer and typographer. The design of Chêneau preserves the space of each letterform and does not use kerning. For a sense of immediacy Lyons Italic was drawn quickly in one sitting with little editing. There are four Italic ampersands, three in Lyons, and one in Chêneau Italic. Chêneau has ligatures and text figures and the small capital font includes titling figures.

Work
Statement

TypeDirectorsClub
TDC² 2000 Winners

TDC 46+ P.293

Blue Island

Design_Jeremy Tankard,
United Kingdom

Type Foundry_Adobe Systems

ABCDÐEFGHIJKLŁMNOPQRSTUVWXYZÞ
abcdðefghijklłmnopqrstuvwxyzþ&@ªº
1234567890Ø¹²³¼½¾£$¢¥€ƒ¤%‰
ŒÆÁÀÄÂÃÅÇÉÈËÊÍÌÏÎÑÓÒÖÔÕØŠÚÙÜÛÝŸŽ
œæáàäâãåçéèëêfiflíìïîñóòöôõøßšúùüûµýÿž
?!¿¡([{}]):;.,'""„…‹«»§¶†‡*±÷×+−=<>^/\|¦#•¯˘˙˚¨˜¸˝˛ˇ©®™

Es eS cages

Southëastèrly vëerîng sõüthwèsterly 6 tö gãle 8, beçomïng cýcl

Vikìng. Šøuthérlý 3 iñcreåšing 5 õr 6. Fãïr.

Thåmës. Wéšterlý bạckiñg southwesterly

føg pàtçhes

Costa

Design_Jean-François Porchez, France

Type Foundry_Porchez Typofonderie for Costa Crociere_Landor Associates, Paris

Family_Light, Regular, Italic, Bold, Logotype

Costa
Costa
Costa
Costa

abcdefghijklmnop
qrstuvwxyzgðłþæ
œfiflßABCDEFGHI
JKLMNOPQRSTUV
WXYZŁÐÆŒ&01
23456789$¥¢£€f@
!?([{/%½¼«",.#¶§†‡*

COSTA IS A CORPORATE TYPEFACE DESIgned for Costa Crociere. The new typeface, developed in conjunction with Landor Associates is used by Costa Crociere for all their publications, from website, catalogs, corporate leaflets to annual reports, etc. The typeface is developed in four styles. Available for the retail market through Porchez Typofonderie in 2003. *Costa est un caractère typographique d'identité visuelle conçu pour Costa Crociere. Ce nouveau caractère, développé en conjonction avec Landor Asso-*ciates, **est utilisé par Costa Crociere pour l'ensemble de leurs publications, de leur**

Erica Sans

Design_Yanek Iontef
Israel

Type Foundry_Iontef Type Foundry

Script_Hebrew

אבגדהוזחטיכלמנסעפצקר
שתרםןףץ 1234567890
(%₪#$☆;:!?)

אבגדהוזחטיכלמנסעפצק
רשתרםןףץ 1234567890
(%₪#$☆;:!?)

אבגדהוזחטיכלמנסע
פצקרשתרםןףץ
(%₪$☆;:!?)1234567890

Homemade

Design_Takaya Goto, USA
Takashi Konuma, Japan

Type Foundry_Oxygen Design

Family_Regular, Rough

Script_Japanese

カスタード
ピーナツバター
シークレットレシピ
スウィートホイップクリーム
フレッシュベイクトチョコレートチップクッキー

ホームメイド
アイウエオカキクケコサシスセソタチツテトナニヌネノハヒフヘホ
マミムメモヤユヨラリルレロワヲンガギグゲゴザジズゼゾヴダヂ
ヅデドバビブベボパピプペポァィゥェォャュョッツー／、。・'()「」!?

ホームメイド・ラフ
アイウエオカキクケコサシスセソタチツテトナニヌネノハヒフヘホ
マミムメモヤユヨラリルレロワヲンガギグゲゴザジズゼゾヴダヂ
ヅデドバビブベボパピプペポァィゥェォャュョッツー／、。・'()「」!?

Design_Gayaneh Bagdasaryan, Russia   **Type Foundry**_ParaType

Scripts_Cyrillic, Latin

Design_Gabriel Martinez Meave
Mexico

Family_Roman, Italic

ABCDEFGHIJKLMNOPQRSTUVWXYZ
abcdefghijklmnopqrstuvwxyz
АБВГДЕЁЖЗИЙКЛМНОПРСТУФХЦЧШ
ЩЪЫЬЭЮЯабвгдеёжзийклмнопрст
уфхцчшщъыыьюэя(1234567890).,:;!?
{№.$¢£¥¶}*-„''""†&ÇçŒÆœæ•«®§©»

ABCDEFGHIJKLMNOPQRSTUVWXYZ
abcdefghijklmnopqrstuvwxyz
АБВГДЕЁЖЗИЙКЛМНОПРСТУФХЦЧШ
ЩЪЫЬЭЮЯабвгдеёжзийклмнопрст
уфхцчшщъыыьюэя(1234567890).,:;!?
{№.$¢£¥¶}*-„''""†&ÇçŒÆœæ•«®§©»

قال الله جَلَّ جَلالُه في كتابه العزيز في الآيات الأخيرة من سورة يونس عَلَيهِ السَّلام :

بِسْمِ اللّهِ الرَّحْمَنِ الرَّحِيمِ

وَإِن يَمْسَسْكَ اللّهُ بِضُرٍّ فَلاَ كَاشِفَ لَهُ إِلاَّ هُوَ وَإِن يُرِدْكَ بِخَيْرٍ فَلاَ رَآدَّ لِفَضْلِهِ يُصِيبُ بِهِ مَن يَشَاءُ مِنْ عِبَادِهِ وَهُوَ الْغَفُورُ الرَّحِيمُ ۝ قُلْ يَا أَيُّهَا النَّاسُ قَدْ جَاءَكُمُ الْحَقُّ مِن رَّبِّكُمْ فَمَنِ اهْتَدَى فَإِنَّمَا يَهْتَدِي لِنَفْسِهِ وَمَن ضَلَّ فَإِنَّمَا يَضِلُّ عَلَيْهَا وَمَا أَنَاْ عَلَيْكُم بِوَكِيلٍ ۝ وَاتَّبِعْ مَا يُوحَى إِلَيْكَ وَاصْبِرْ حَتَّى يَحْكُمَ اللّهُ وَهُوَ خَيْرُ الْحَاكِمِينَ ۝

صدق الله العظيم

Myriad Greek

Design_Carol Twombly and
Robert Slimbach, USA

Type Foundry_Adobe Systems

Style_Light, Regular, Semibold,
Bold, Black_Roman, Italic (each in
Condensed, Normal and Semi-
extended widths)

Script_Greek

Νομίζω ότι είναι ιδιαίτερα δύσκολο
να δημιουργηθεί μια καινούργια
γραματοσειρά όπως είναι δύσκολο
να δημιουργηθεί ένα καινούργιο
ο, τιδήποτε που χρησιμοποιείται
καθημερινα. Η δημιουργία μιας
νέα γραματοσειράς αντιστοιχεί σε
ενα καινούργιο κομάτι μουσικής.

26/33 LIGHT, REGULAR, SEMIBOLD, BOLD BLACK AND ITALICS

ΑΛΦΆΒΗΤΟΥ

87PT BLACK CONDENSED

σημαντικό

12PT LIGHT CONDENSED

Νομίζω ότι είναι ιδιαίτερα δύσκολο να δημιουργηθεί
μια καινούργια γραματοσειρά όπως είναι δύσκολο
να δημιουργηθεί ένα καινούργιο ο, τιδήποτε που
χρησιμοποιείται καθημερινα. Η δημιουργία μιας νέα
γραματοσειράς αντιστοιχεί σε ένα καινούργιο κομάτι

10/12 LIGHT SEMI-EXTENDED, LIGHT SEMI-EXTENDED ITALIC

Νομίζω ότι είναι ιδιαίτερα δύσκολο να δημιουργηθεί
μια καινούργια γραματοσειρά όπως είναι δύσκολο
να δημιουργηθεί ένα καινούργιο ο, τιδήποτε που
χρησιμοποιείται καθημερινα. Η δημιουργία μιας νέα
γραματοσειράς αντιστοιχεί σε ένα καινούργιο κομάτι

10/12 SEMIBOLD SEMI-EXTENDED, SEMI-EXTENDED ITALIC

Νομίζω ότι είναι ιδιαίτερα δύσκολο να
δημιουργηθεί μια καινούργια γραματοσειρά όπως
είναι δύσκολο να δημιουργηθεί ένα καινούργιο
ο, τιδήποτε που χρησιμοποιείται καθημερινα. Η
δημιουργία μιας νέα γραματοσειράς αντιστοιχεί σε

10/12 SEMIBOLD SEMI-EXTENDED, SEMIBOLD SEMI-EXT ITALIC

Νομίζω ότι είναι ιδιαίτερα δύσκολο να
δημιουργηθεί μια καινούργια γραματοσειρά όπως
είναι δύσκολο να δημιουργηθεί ένα καινούργιο ο.
τιδήποτε που χρησιμοποιείται καθημερινα. Η

10/12 BOLD SEMI-EXTENDED, BOLD SEMI-EXTENDED ITALIC

Νομίζω ότι είναι ιδιαίτερα δύσκολο να
δημιουργηθεί μια καινούργια γραματοσειρά όπως
είναι δύσκολο να δημιουργηθεί ένα καινούργιο ο,
τιδήποτε που χρησιμοποιείται καθημερινα. Η

10/12 BLACK SEMI-EXTENDED, BLACK SEMI-EXTENDED ITALIC

305

Nani

Design_Charles Nix, USA
(ornaments by Stefano Arcella)

Type Foundry_New Fonts

FF Profile

Design_Martin Wenzel,
The Netherlands

Type Foundry_FSI FontShop
International

Style_Light, Regular, Medium,
Bold, Black_ Roman, Italic

(each in Normal, SC, No and Xp
character sets)

WOMEN COME AND GO talking of Xxx. *Yearning*
toward Zero. **ALTHOUGH thy hand and faith
By *children's* births, and death,** Could make
me any summer's story tell. *DEATH is like
the insect,* Exhuberant, restless, Flesh of his
excavated flesh. Glory is that *bright tragic
thing,* HOLY the groaning saxophone! I have
nourish'd the wounded Journeyers with their
own sublime Knowing. Let us go then, you
and Me. No coward soul is mine. OH, LET ME
OUT! Prison and palace and reverberation,
Quoth the Raven, nevermore. *Some say good-
night at night,* The riddle we can guess, Unto
me? Violence leaped and appeared in the
room the *WOMEN COME AND GO talking of Xxx.*

aɑAA
aɑAA
aɑAA
aɑAA
aɑAA

a b c d e f g h i j k l m n o p
q r s t u v w x y z 0 1 2 3 4 5
6 7 8 9 A B C D E F G H I J K L
M N O P Q R S T U V W X Y Z 0 1
2 3 4 5 6 7 8 9 a b c d e f g h
i j k l m n o p q r s t u v w x y
z ꝫ @á à â ä ã å 0 1 2 3 4 5 6
7 8 9 ¹₁²₂³₃⁴₄⁵₅⁶₆⁷₇⁸₈⁹₉⁰₀ ¢ € € ƒ £ £
$ $ ¥ ¥ ¶ & & ?? !! § # ©)] } ← *

[Ypsilon kam hier noch gar nicht dabei...]

MONTAG NACHT: 2.36 Uhr. Typografen schlafen
nicht? (Nicht bei £140,–/h) Doch, aber nur selten
wenn es dunkel ist (*"Schazile, es is schoh gans
negadiv drœse."*). Der Enthusiasmus hält sie wach
und aufmerksam. Der Inhalt von Geschriebenem
verschwindet hinter der Form, dem Bild einzelner
Buchstaben oder dem ganzer typografischer
Landschaften.

Die Euphorie, sich STUNDENLANG in Welten von
allerkleinsten Einheiten zu bewegen, ist für *andere*
meist nicht nachvollziehbar. **Selbst bei** *"Dißäner"*-
Kollegen ist *DIESE Lust* **am Wort** *leider* **nicht so etc.**

Design_ Jovica Veljović,
Yugoslavia/Germany

Silentium Pro

Type Foundry_Adobe Systems

Style_Roman I, Roman II

KNAPSACK

ADDITIONAL CHARACTERS- ROMAN I

ABCDEFGGHIJKLMNOPQRRSTTUV
WXYZ ABCDEFGHIJKLMNOPQRSTUVWXYZ&01234567
890 !?¡¿ $£¥€ ÆŒÞFIFLSS AEGMMPQRTaaeegiiorrfttvw !?¡¿
A'GEEGEGGDDHFRLMNKOØØØOTTiTöTTVEÆEÐP æœčtęxgg
fafbfffffifffiflflfhfifkflfjfrftftfðrartshspštтatttytzzzßþð
(¼¼½¾%‰/°) [#$¢£€ƒ¥¤] {¥} ao1234 1234ℓ℮∂∏∑μπ√∞∫^=÷×+–¬
±<>~≈≠≤≥◊§†‡¶¶* .,:;'"'"',.....•«»o---—_\/|¡@©®™ 𝒴❦

ACCENTED CHARACTERS- ROMAN I

āăąáâàäåãćçd'dèéęéêëèğ̆ğīíîïïiķĺľļłñńňņôõöòôòòøŕřŗśşšťṭúũų̇ų̈ú
úûüùýÿżžż ´ˆˋ¨˜˙¸˝˛ˇ ̣ÀĂĄÁÂÄÅÃĆČÇDÈĔĘÉÊËÈĞĞĪÍÎ
ĨĬKĹĽĻŁÑŃŇŅÔÕÖÒÔÒÒØŔŘŖŚŞŠŤṬÚŨŲŲ́ÚÛÜÙÝŸZ
ŻŻ ÀĂĄÁÂÄÅÃĆČÇDÐÈĔĘÉÊËÈĞĞĪĨ Í Î Ĩ Ĭ Ì Ķ Ĺ Ľ Ļ Ł Ŀ Ñ Ń Ň Ņ
ÔÕÖÒÔÒÒØ ŔŘŖŚŞŠŤṬÚŨŲŲ́ÚÛÜÙÝŸŹŽŻ

24 (30PT) ORNAMENTS

▨▨◪◪▧◫◫▤▭▥▤▨▤▦◩◪▧▧▧▨▦▨▤▨

Here is sanctity which shames
our religions, & reality which
discredits our heroes. Here we
find nature to be the circumstance which dwarfs every
other circumstance, and judges like
a god all men that come to her. We
have crept out of our close and
crowded houses into the night and
morning, and we see what majestic
beauties daily wrap us in their bosom.
How willingly we would escape the
barriers which render them compara-
tively impotent, escape the sophistication
and second thought, and suffer nature to
entrance us. The tempered light of the woods
is like a perpetual morning, and is stimulat-
ing and heroic. The anciently reported spells
of these places creep on us. The stems of

Linotype Syntax

Design_Hans Eduard Meier,
Switzerland

Type Foundry_Linotype Library
GmbH

Style_Light, Regular,
Medium_Roman, Italic (each in
Normal, SC and OsF character sets)

Bold, Heavy, Black_Roman, Italic
(each in Normal and OsF character
sets)

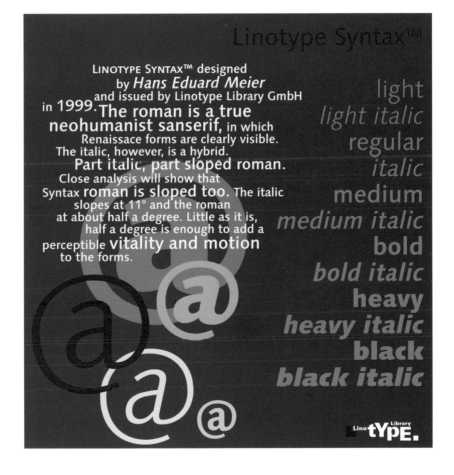

+

TypeDirectorsClub
Board Members / Typographic Index
General Index

Board of Directors 1999/2000

Officers
President — Mark Solsburg, DsgnHaus, Inc.
Vice President — Gerard Huerta, Gerard Huerta Design, Inc.
Secretary/Treasurer — Daniel Pelavin

Directors-at-Large
Syndi Becker, Money Magazine
John Berry
Ronn Campisi, Ronn Campisi Design
Susan Cotler-Block, Fashion Institute of Technology
David Cundy, Design Trust, Inc.
James Montalbano, Terminal Design
Ina Saltz, Golf Magazine
Maxim Zhukov, The United Nations

Executive Director — Carol Wahler

Board of Directors 2000/2001

Officers
President — Daniel Pelavin
Secretary/Treasurer — James Montalbano, Terminal Design, Inc.

Directors-at-Large
John Berry
Ronn Campisi, Ronn Campisi Design
Matthew Carter, Carter & Cone
Allan Haley, Resolution
Gary Munch, MunchFonts
Louise Fili, Louise Fili Ltd.
Ina Saltz, Golf Magazine
Maxim Zhukov, United Nations

Chairman — Mark Solsburg, DsgnHaus, Inc.
Executive Director — Carol Wahler

Committee for TDC46

Chairperson — Susan Cotler-Block
Design — ATTIK
Coordinator — Carol Wahler
Assistant Coordinator — Klaus Schmidt

Assistants to Judges
Abigail Arafeli	Rosemary	Agatha Sohn
Peter Bain	Markowsky	Martin Solomon
John Berry	Lawrence Mirsky	Mark Solsburg
Deborah Gonet	James Montalbano	Allan R. Wahler
Gerard Huerta	Eric Neuner	Samantha Wahler
Nathalie Kirsheh	Alexa Nosal	Matt Weber
Nana Kobayashi	Daniel Pelavin	

Type Directors Club Presidents

Frank Powers, 1946, 1947
Milton Zudeck, 1948
Alfred Dickman, 1949
Joseph Weiler, 1950
James Secrest, 1951, 1952, 1953
Gustave Saelens, 1954, 1955
Arthur Lee, 1956, 1957
Martin Connell, 1958
James Secrest, 1959, 1960
Frank Powers, 1961, 1962
Milton Zudeck, 1963, 1964
Gene Ettenberg, 1965, 1966
Edward Gottschall, 1967, 1968
Saadyah Maximon, 1969
Louis Lepis, 1970, 1971
Gerard O'Neill, 1972, 1973
Zoltan Kiss, 1974, 1975
Roy Zucca, 1976, 1977
William Streever, 1978, 1979
Bonnie Hazelton, 1980, 1981
Jack George Tauss, 1982, 1983
Klaus F. Schmidt, 1984, 1985
John Luke, 1986, 1987
Jack Odette, 1988, 1989
Ed Benguiat, 1990, 1991
Allan Haley, 1992, 1993
B. Martin Pedersen, 1994, 1995
Mara Kurtz, 1996, 1997
Mark Solsburg, 1998, 1999
Daniel Pelavin, 2000

TDC Medal Recipients

Hermann Zapf, 1967
R. Hunter Middleton, 1968
Frank Powers, 1971
Dr. Robert Leslie, 1972
Edward Rondthaler, 1975
Arnold Bank, 1979
Georg Trump, 1982
Paul Standard, 1983
Herb Lubalin, 1984 (posthumously)
Paul Rand, 1984
Aaron Burns, 1985
Bradbury Thompson, 1986
Adrian Frutiger, 1987
Freeman Craw, 1988
Ed Benguiat, 1989
Gene Federico, 1991
Lou Dorfsman, 1995
Matthew Carter, 1997
Rolling Stone magazine, 1997
Colin Brignall, 2000
Günter Gerhard Lange, 2000

Special Citations to TDC Members

Edward Gottschall, 1955
Freeman Craw, 1968
James Secrest, 1974
Olaf Leu, 1984, 1990
William Streever, 1984
Klaus F. Schmidt, 1985
John Luke, 1987
Jack Odette, 1989

2000 Scholarship Recipients

Brian J. Hoffer,
The Cooper Union School of Art
Pei Wen Sharon Goh,
Pratt Institute
Beom Seok Kim,
School of Visual Arts
Paul T. Reid,
Art Center College of Design
Eugene Rogovitz,
Fashion Institute of Technology
Alejandra Santos,
Parsons School of Design
Philipp Arnold,
Hochschule für Grafik und Buckkunst Leipzig

**International
Liaison
Chairpersons**

AUSTRALIA
Mark Simkins
Simkins & Smart
Suite 3, 6-7 Gurrigal Street
Mosman, Sydney 2088

ENGLAND
David Farey
HouseStyle Graphics
31 Clerkenwell Close
London EC1R 0AT

FRANCE
Christopher Dubber
Signum Art
94, Avenue Victor Hugo
94100 Saint Maur Des Fosses

GERMANY
Bertram Schmidt-Friderichs
Universitatsdruckerei und Verlag
H. Schmidt GmbH & Co.
Robert Koch Strasse 8
Postfach 42 07 28
55129 Mainz Hechtsheim

JAPAN
Zempaku Suzuki
Japan Typography Association
Sanukin Bldg. 5 Fl.
1-7-10 Nihonbashi-honcho
Chuo-ku, Toyko 104-0041

MEXICO
Prof. Felix Beltran
Apartado de Correos
M 10733 Mexico 06000

SOUTH AMERICA
Diego Vainesman
Punto Sur, Inc.
420 East 79 Street, #4B
New York, New York 10021

SWEDEN
Ernst Dernehl
Dernehl & Son Designers
Box 8073
S-10420 Stockholm

SWITZERLAND
Eric Alb
Syndor Press
Lindenbühl 33
CH 6330 Cham

VIETNAM
Richard Moore
21 Bond Street
New York, NY 10012

Type Directors Club
60 East 42nd Street
Suite 721
New York, NY 10165
212-983-6042 FAX: 212-983-6043
E-mail: director@tdc.org
www.tdc.org

Carol Wahler, Executive Director
For membership information,
please contact the
Type Directors Club office.

312

A Marcelle Accardi '98s
Debbie Adams '98
Jim Aitchison '93
Eric Alb '96
Jack Anderson '96
Martyn Anstice '92
Don Ariev '98s
Jenna Ashley '97
Jeffrey Austin '98
B Jaques Bagios '95
Peter Bain '86
Boris Balant '99
Bruce Balkin '93
Kevin Balluf '99
Stephen Banham '95
Maria Helena Ferreira Braga
Barbosa '93s
David Barrineau '96
Lucy Bartholomay '96
Barbara Baumann '96
Gerd Baumann '95
Clarence Baylis '74
Chris Bean '00
Lisa Beaudoin '96s
Daniel Garcia Becerril '98s
Syndi Becker '96
Felix Beltran '88
Ed Benguiat '64
Anna Berkenbusch '89
John Berry '96
Peter Bertolami '69
Davide Bevilacqua '99
Klaus Bietz '93
Henrik Birvig '96
Roger Black '80
Alan Boarts '96
Barbara A. Boccio '99
Karlheinz Boelling '86
Garrett Boge '83
Matteo Bologna '00
John Bonadies '95
Marguerita Bornstein-Fahrer '96
Gianni Bortolotti '98
Jamie Boyle '99
Patricia Bradbury '93
Fred Brady '97
Bud Braman '90
Ulrike Brenner '99
Ed Brodsky '80
Andreas Brunlinghaus '97s
Bill Bundzak '64
Ulrich Burgdorf '96
Queenie Burns '94
Sara Burris '97
Thomas F. Burroughs '00
Steve Byers '98
C Lynn Cabot-Puris '99
Joanne Cadovius '99s
Casandra Calo '98s
Ronn Campisi '88
Diane Carrier '98
Matthew Carter '88
Steve Cassar '96
Tony Castellano '97
Ken Cato '88
Paul Caullettt '98s
Amy H. N. Chan '96s

Eric Chan '97
Theseus Chan '94
Jennie Chano '99
David Chaves '96
Len Cheeseman '93
David Cheung, Jr. '98
Heung-Heung Chin '98s
Kai-Yan Choi '90
Kyong Choi '96s
Stanley Church '97
Traci Churchill '95
Sheri Cifaldi '97s
John V. Clarke '99
Travis Cliett '53
Graham Clifford '98
Mahlon A. Cline* '48
Tom Cocozza '76
Lisa Cohen '93
Stuart Cohen '96
Angelo Colella '90
Ed Colker '83
Kyle Cooper '97
Rodrigo Corral '98
Madeleine Corson '96
Lynette Cortez '99
Susan Cotler-Block '89
Freeman Craw* '47
Laura Crookston '00
Bart Crosby '95
Ray Cruz '00
Jeff Culver '97s
David Cundy '85
Brian Cunningham '96
Rick Cusick '89
D Michael Damare '98
Ziya Danishmend '00
Susan Darbyshire '87
Richard Dawson '93
Einat Lisa Day '97s
Matej Decko '93
Paige De Leo '98
Josanne De Natale '86
Phil Delbourgo '98
Margi Denton '99
Ernst Dernehl '87
Meir Deutsch '00s
Roberto de Vicq de Cumptich '97
W. Brian Diecks '98
Claude A. Dieterich '84
Joseph DiGioia '96
Jeanette Wilkinson Dill '99
Tom Dolle '95
Jonathan Doney '96
Lou Dorfsman '54
Pascale Dovic '97
Stephen Doyle '98
John Dreyfus** '68
Christopher Dubber '85
Rod Durso '98
Simon Dwelly '98
Lutz Dziarnowski '92
Lasko Dzurovski '00
E Friedrich Eisenmenger '93
Jeani Eismont '96
Lise Ellingson '98s
Dr. Elsi Vassdal Ellis '93
Garry Emery '93

Elke Erschfeld '99
Rafael Esquer '00
Joseph Michael Essex '78
Leslie Evans '92
Florence Everett '89
F John Fahey '98s
Peter Fahrni '93
Joihn Fairley '00
Dug Falby '99
John R. Falker '00
David Farey '93
Michael Farmer '94
Erik Faulhaber '97s
Sean Fermoyle '00
Antero Ferreira '97
Louise Fili '00
Simon Fitton '94
Kristine Fitzgerald '90
Gonçalo Fonseca '93
Wayne Ford '96
Margaret Kane Forgosh '99
Thomas Fowler '93
Alessandro Franchini '96
George Frederick '00
Carol Freed '87
Tobias Frere-Jones '00
Adrian Frutiger ** '67
Mario Fuhr '97
G Christopher Galvin '99s
Christof Gassner '90
Martina Gates '96s
David Gatti '81
Matthew Gaynor '00s
Jeremy Gee '93
Kai Gehrmann '96s
Robyn Gill-Attaway '93
Lou Glassheim * '47
Howard Glener '77
Rüdiger Goetz '95
Carin Goldberg '97
Lorenz Goldnagl '99s
Ronnen Goren '97
Holly Goscinsky '98s
Edward Gottschall '52
Norman Graber '69
Diana Graham '85
Austin Grandjean '59
Stefanie Grashoff '99s
Stephen Green '97
Karen Greenberg '95
Adam Greiss '89
Ariel Grey '00
James Grieshaber '96
Jeff Griffith '91
Frank E.E. Grubich '96
Rosanne Guararra '92
Grace Guarte '00s
Christiane Gude '97
Stefan Guggenbichler '97
Sandra Gulla '00
Olga Gutierrez de la Roza '95s
Einar Gylfason '95
Peter Gyllan '97
H Doug Haden '97
William Hafeman '96
Allan Haley '78
Crystal Hall '97

Debra Hall '96
Egil Haraldsen '00
Keith Harris '98
Theodore Harrison '96
Knut Hartmann '85
Helen Hayes '98
Bonnie Hazelton '75
Jeri Heiden '94
Frank Heine '96
Wild Heinz '96
Earl M. Herrick '96
Klaus Hesse '95
Michael Heu '00s
Eric Heupel '00s
Fons M. Hickmann '96
Jay Higgins '88
Helmut Himmler '96
Norihiko Hirata '96
J. Drew Hodges '95
Michael Hodgson '89
Jonathan Hoefler '00
Fritz Hofrichter '80
Troy Holder '99
Catherine Hollenbeck '93
Roman Holt '99
Kevin Horvath '87
Tonya Hudson '99
Gerard Huerta '85
David Hukari '95
Harvey Hunt '92
I Yanek Iontef '00
Terry Irwin '96
J Donald Jackson ** '78
Michael Jager '94
Mark Jamra '99
Andy Johnson '99
Iskra Johnson '94
Margo Johnson '99
K Otso Kallinen '00
John Kallio '96
Rosanne Kang '98
Kelly Kao '98
Maryann Karr Saggese '96
Carolyn Kaufman '99
Ronan Keane '99
Nan Keeton '97
Brunnette Kenan '99
Kay Khoo '99
Jang Hoon Kim '97s
Linda S. Kim '98
Rick King '93
Richard King '00
Brandie Kirkman '98s
Alexander Knowlton '96
Cynthia Knox '95
Nana Kobayashi '94
Akira Kobayashi '99
Claus Koch '96
Jesse Taylor Koechling '98s
Daniel Kolcinsky '99s
Steve Kopec '74
Matthias Kott '96s
Katharina Kramer '99s
Andrej Krátky '93
Marcus Kraus '97
Philip Krayna '97
Bernhard J. Kress '63

Helvetica Black_068
Max Miedinger

Helvetica Neue_26, 100, 183
Linotype after Max Miedinger

Neue Helvetica 55 Roman
Max Medinger

Helvetica Neue Medium_256
Linotype after Max Miedinger

Hiragino Gyosho Extra Bold_045
Dai Nippon Screen Co., Ltd.

HTF Hoefler Engraved_145
Jonathan Hoefler

HonMincho_106
Ryobi Limited

I Industrial 736 (Torino)_223
Alessandro Butti

Interstate_083, 097, 168, 192, 196, 213, 253
Tobias Frere-Jones

Interstate Bold_098
Tobias Frere-Jones

FF Isonorm_081
Robert Kirchnert

J Adobe Jenson_259
Robert Slimbach based on design by Nicolas Jenson and Ludovico degli Arrighi

Jigsaw_080
Elliott Earles

Joanna_120
Eric Gill

Jurriaan Square_262
Leonardo Sonnoli

K Kabello Extra Bold_173
after Kabel by Rudolf Koch

Keedy Sans_101
Jeffery Keedy

Key Stone State_056
Anuthin Wongsunkakon

FF Kipp_206
Claude Kipp

ITC Kokoa_045
Jochen Schuss

Künstler Script_082, 250
Hans Bohn

L La Mummia_227
Eric Cruz and Mike Jakab

Letter Gothic_147, 154
Roger Robertson

Leucadia_092
Betsy Kopshina and Rodney S. Fehsenfeld

Linotext_073
Morris Fuller Benton

Lunatix_118
Zuzana Licko

M Morisawa MB 101_123
Minao Tsukada

Morisawa MB 31
unknown

FB Magneto Bold_092
Leslie Cabarga

FB Magneto Bold Extended_092
Leslie Cabarga

FB Magneto Super Bold_092
Leslie Cabarga

Malcy.1_059
Malcolm Buick

Mason_104
Jonathan Barnbrook

Matrix Bold_24
Zuzana Licko

Melior_247
Hermann Zapf

FF Meta_066
Erik Spiekermann

Metamorphosis_056
Anuthin Wongsunkakon

Microscan_240
unknown

Midwest Federal_182
Tom Eslinger

Minaret_090
MacKellar, Smiths & Jordan

Monoline Script_036, 153
unknown

Monospace Bold_158
unknown

Mrs. Eaves_080, 081, 145, 166, 175, 192
Zuzana Licko

N News Gothic_038, 047, 091, 105, 135
Morris Fuller Benton

Monotype News Gothic_126, 127
John Renshaw after Morris Fuller Benton

Nobel_055, 136
Tobias Frere Jones after S.H. deRoos

Not Caslon_030
Mark Andresen

NZSO Non Regular_212
Hayden Doughty

O OCR B_137
Adrian Frutiger

OCRBuero_121
unknown

CIA Oddjob_221
Jens Gehlhaar

ITC Officina_121, 168
Erik Spiekermann

ITC Officina Sans_261
Erik Spiekermann

Orator_054, 136, 154, 158, 216
L. H. D. Smit

P Pastis Nobel_051
Tamaye Parry

Pastis Rockwell_051
Tamaye Parry

Pastis Geometric Slab Condensed_051
Tamaye Parry

Perpetua_069, 083, 104
Eric Gill

Puzzle_117
Katsunori Nishi

R Rechtmann Script_236
Helmut Himmler and Judith Treder

Rosewood_090, 126, 127
Kim Buker Chansler, Carl Crossgrove, and Carol Twombly

Rosewood Fill_073
Kim Buker Chansler, Carl Crossgrove, and Carol Twombly

Russell Square_055
John Russell

S Sackers Gothic_190
Agfa Design Staff

FF Scala Sans_147, 243
Martin Majoor

FF Scratch_046
Max Kisman

Schneider-Antiqua_28
Werner Schneider

Schwere_036, 153
after H. Berthold AG

Section_097
Greg Lindy

Shelley_109
Alan Meeks

Seibold_108
J. Otto Seibold

ITC Snap Italic_045
David Sagnorski

Son Gothic_056, 186
Anuthin Wongsunkakon

Space_116
unknown

Starro_182
Tom Eslinger

Stempel Schneidler_141
F. H. Ernst Schneidler

Subluxation_080
Elliott Earles

T Tear Drop_065, 075
Shuichi Nogami

Texas Hero_073
after handwritten letters of Thomas Jefferson Rusk and other Texas heroes

TheSans_218
Luc(as) de Groot

FF Thesis_046
Luc(as) de Groot

Times New Roman_032, 078, 222, 258, 263, 264
Stanley Morison and Victor Lardent

Trade Gothic_32, 33, 055, 057, 062, 071, 079, 083, 084, 092, 096, 102, 112, 114, 129, 145, 148, 155, 161, 178, 224, 229, 237, 258, 260
Jackson Burke

Trade Gothic Condensed_159
Jackson Burke

Trinité_167
Bram de Does

Triumvirate (Helvetica)_079, 129, 161
Compugraphic staff

Twentieth Century_043
based on Futura after Paul Renner

Typewriter_078
unknown

U Univers_055, 062, 069, 070, 094, 103, 119, 120, 133, 151, 155, 163, 197, 215, 230
Adrian Frutiger

Univers Black Extended_156
Adrian Frutiger

Univers Condensed_228, 247
Adrian Frutiger

Univers Extended_135, 163
Adrian Frutiger

Univers Extra Black_245
Adrian Frutiger

Univers 55_119
Adrian Frutiger

V V.A.G. Rounded_239
unknown

Monotype Van Dijck_230
Jan Van Krimpen after Christoffel van Dijck

Variex_069, 273
Rudy VanderLans and Zuzana Licko

Vendetta_064
John Downer

W Walker_267
Matthew Carter

ITC Weidemann_091
Kurt Weidemann

Windows OS System Fixed Font_238
unknown

Worm Hole_160, 252
Katsunori Nishi

Z Zentenar-Fraktur_141
F. H. Ernst Schneidler

BT Zurich (Univers)_111, 255
Adrian Frutiger

16 X 16 Visual User Interface Design_240
2D3D_203
2wice Arts Foundation_243
4th Estate_144
5D Studio_240

A Achituv, Romy_238
Ackerman, Elizabeth_114
Ackroyd, Tom_212
Adam D. Tihany International, Ltd._219
Adobe Systems_294, 295, 305, 308
Akgulian, Nishan_081
Aki, Kenichi_244
Al-Saadi, Hamid_304
Alicino, Christine_137
Amaguri-Taro, Inc._045
American Institute of Graphic Arts, Detroit_265
American Institute of Graphic Arts/ Chicago_132
American Institute of Graphic Design/Minnesota_047
American Printing History Association_141
AND_108, 242
Anderson, Charles S._037, 062, 155, 171
Ando bv_203
Andresevic, Jill_195
Anni Kuan Design_194
Apeloig Design_245
Apeloig, Philippe_245
appleby, bobby_205
Appleton Papers_202
Arafeli, Abigail_118
Arcella, Stefano_306
Archetype Press at Art Center College of Design_232
Art Center College of Design_232
Art Directors Association of Iowa_044
Art Force Studio_049
Arthesia_202
Atelier Paxion_222
Atelier Poisson_079, 129, 161
Attik_004, 012, 031
Attila, Simon_049
Auclair, Marijoac_105
Aufuldish, Bob_202

B B.J. Krivanek Art+Design_158
Bach, Isabel_138
Bacino, Brian_190
Bagdasaryan, Gayanch_301
Baglee, Patrick_255
Bain, Peter_141
The Bang_032, 258, 260, 263, 264
Bargmann, Richard_170
Barminski, Bill_130
Barnathan, Michael_217
Baseman, Frank_082
Bathgate, Alec_259
Bauer, Joerg_224
BDO Stoy Hayward/Kite (UK) Limited_104
Beckerle, Matthew_247
Belkowitz, Steve_105
Bernard, Walter_211
Besson, Luc_226
Bibb, Daniel_228
Bichler, Paul_041
Bielenberg Design_202
Bielenberg, John_202
Bierut, Michael_064, 098, 235
Bink_108

Birnbach Design_046
Birnbach, Heribert_046
Bittner, Patrick_138
Black + White magazine_250
Blattner, Wendy_126, 127
Blok Design_084, 096
Blonde Magazine_247
Blue Q_107
Bluey, Ted_043, 197
Bluming, Adam_209
Bockting, Hans_167, 203
Bogner, S. _116
Bologna, Matteo Federico_051
Bouchard, Gilles_222
Bowden, Jason_212
Boxheimer, Jutta_072
Boyko-Hrushetsky, Halyna_024
Boynton, Richard_191
Bradley, Gavin_212
Brahman Company Limited_117, 160, 252
Brainard, Kevin_148
Breaux, Joel _158
Brewer, Allen _135
Bridges, Betty_208
Briere, Alain_195
Brigitte, Tartière_222
Broad, Julian_022
Brooklyn Law School_145
Brooks, Roy_243
Brown, Malcolm_256
Brown, Tom_063
Bryant, Keith_195, 201
Bryant, Seri_226
Buck, Chris_124
Buick_188
Buick, Malcolm_059
Burk, Jennifer_175
Büro Hamburg JK.PW._121
Büro Uebele_072
Buttrem, Melba_208
Buzz Magazine_266
Byrne, David_237

C C.J. Graphics_169, 178
Cadillac_220
Cahan & Associates_020, 124, 130, 137
Cahan, Bill_020, 124, 130, 137
Calero, Anita_142
California State University_158
Candace Gelman & Associates_162
Canning, Scott_209
Cannon, David_110
Carmichael Lynch Thorburn_239
Carr, Daniel_290
Carter, Matthew_277, 278, 284
Casado, John_030
Champagne, Amie_133, 215
Champion International_055, 136, 147
Chan Wing Kei, Leslie_060
Chao, Larcher_060
Character_254
Charles S. Anderson Design_037, 062, 155, 171
Chavez, Johnny_263
Checkowski, Matt_217, 220
Cheeseman, Len_212
Chen, Frances_084, 096
Chicago Department of Cultural Affairs_024
Chin, Justin_060
Chip Kidd Design_010
Chmiel, P.J._062
Chronicle Books_254
Chung, Stephen_256

Cité du Livre, Aix-en-Provence_245
Clawson, Abby_026, 142
Clayton, David_209
Code, Traci_174
Collateral Therapeutics_137
Colquhoun, David_182, 212
Columbia Artists_156
Columbia TriStar_226
Columbus, Chris_217
Community Architexts_024
Computerwoche – Verlag I.D.G._261
Concrete Design Communications_169, 178
Consiglio, Jeff_205, 220
Consolidated Papers_030
Cooper, Kyle_190, 201, 227
Corpuz, Victor_240
Costarella, Vittorio_107
Coulter Pharmaceutical_124
Coupe_032, 033, 258, 260
Covell, David_055, 136
Cox, Erik_202
Crane's_080, 081
Creative Activity Design Company_247
Cotler-Block, Susan_006
Cruz, Andy_064
Cruz, Antonio_183
Cruz, Eric_209, 227
Cullen, Matt_195, 220, 226
CUT magazine/Rockin'on Inc._204

D D'Amore, Venus_030, 077
D'Astolfo, Frank_170
Daigle, Keith_067, 102
Daiminger, Michael_074
DaimlerChrysler AG_022
Dallas Society of Visual Communications_050
Daniel, Sean_227
Davenport, Samantha_110
The David and Alfred Smart Museum of Art_041
Davis, Doug_050
Davy, Sam _184
Dayton's_048, 086
de Groot, Bart_203
de l'Ecluse, Will_167
Dean, Jeremy _061
Dearden, Douglas_108, 242
Deck, Barry_277, 278, 286
DeMartino, Laurie_038, 044, 047, 105
Der, Loid_163
Dervin, Alexander_209, 217, 220, 227
Design: M/W_26, 142, 147
Design Guys_257
DeSocio, Bridget_10, 14, 20
Devendorf, Scott_243
Dieckert, Kurt Georg_22
The Diecks Group, Inc._188
Diecks, Brian_188
Dietz, Aaron_080
Dietz, Kirsten_218
DIG Tokyo Corporation_173
Dimmel, Aaron_044
Dinetz, Bob_020
Diwan Software Ltd._304
Dixon, Doreen_227
DMB&B_220
The Doctor's Company_130
Dolcini Associati_262, 267
Domtar Paper_073
Döring, Iris_225
Doughty, Hayden_212
Douglas Joseph Partners_069

Douglas, Bill_032, 258, 260, 263, 264
Drew, Ned _170
Drueding, Alice_036, 153
Ducsay, Bob_227
Dumbar, Gert_203
Dunjko, Carmen_256
Durrant, Nathan_192
Dzilenski, Liz_081

E EAI_110
Eckstein, Vanessa_084, 096
Ehrich, Eve_188
Eisele, Yael_026, 142
Elhardt, Matt _076
Elixir Design, Inc._192
Elkjer, Thom_020
Eller, Matt_133, 215
Ellis, David_010, 14, 22
Emigre_296
Epstein, Seth_221
Erik Olsen Graphic Design_077
Erler, Johannes_230
Eslinger, Tom_182, 212
Evangelista, Patricia_254
Eveleigh, David_184
Exult_163

F Fachhochschule Düsseldorf_120, 185, 231
Factor Design_039, 052, 149, 230
Factor Product_116
Fahrner, Manus_230
Fairey, Shepard_004
Fairley, John_104
Fallon McElligott_205
Fallon, Andrew_203
Fashion Institute of Technology_118
Fastfood Theater_074
Fauchere, Laurent_220
Feine Werbung_070
Fendley, Tim_184
Fey, Erwin_210
Fisher, Carolyn_081
Professor Gerd Fleischmann_112
Fong, Karin_205
Fong, Steve_190
FontShop Benelux_206
Foote, Cone & Belding_190, 201
Fössel, Katja_225
Fossil Design Studio_168, 175
Foster, Alan_133, 208, 215
Foster, Jeff_076
Fotheringham, Ed_081
Foundation Press_189
Fox, Ken_057, 128
Frailey, Stephen_196
Franceschini, Amy_202
Frank Baseman Design_082
Frankfurt, Peter_195, 205, 209, 217, 226
Fredrik Broden_063
Freie und Hansestadt_207
Freitag-Hild, Lori_201
French Paper Company_037, 047, 062, 105, 155, 171
Friend + Johnson_083
Friends of Rickwood_223
Fringe Ensemble Frank Heuel Theater im Ballsaal_046
Fritsch, Susanne_072
Froeter Design Co., Inc._041, 132
Froeter, Chris_041, 132
Frost Design Ltd._144, 176
Frost, Vince_144, 176
FSI FontShop International_297, 307
Fuel_221
Fukuda, Nob_088
Fukui, Rie_209

Fukumoto, Yasuyo_198, 200
G Galia, Dirk_236
Gallagher Bassett Services Inc._251
Gamulin, Damir_286
Garcia, Elton_227
Garratt, Brenna_163
Garrett, Tom_135
Gassner, Christof_103
Gaudet, Larry_169
Gaylord & Dorothy Donnelley
Foundation_024
Gaz, David_202
Geer Design Inc._073
Geer, Mark_073
Gehlhaar, Jens_221
Gehrke, Frank_261
General Magic_020
Gentl + Hyers_026
Georgia Pacific Papers_110
Gericke, Michael_145
Giordano, Lauren_201, 227
Glasgow 1999_184
Godfrey, Andrew_248, 250
Goldberg, Carin_114, 119, 165
Goldberg, Nathanel _121
Golding, Jono_220, 227
Golf Magazine_012
Golgonooza Letter Foundry
& Press_290
Gondell, Robert_201
Goodman, Emily_227
Goodman, Jim_227
Goto, Takaya_300
Götz, Silja_225
Graff, Jason_209
Graphic Behaviour_056, 186
Gray, Colin_22
Greater Alabama Council_180
Greulich, Rolf_236
Gürtler, Uli_207
Gustavson, Jon_220
Guterl, Fred_253
H Häberlein & Mauerer_116
Hagenberg, Prof. Helfried_120
Hagmann, Sibylle_296
Hakansson, Mats_026, 142, 147
Hale, Tim_168, 175
Hall, Peter_064
Haller, Mischa_022
Hames, Kyle_062, 155
Handschuh, David_078
Hanson, Eric_135
Harding, Andreas_184
Harley-Davidson Motor
Company_057, 128
Harrington, Kimberly_133
Hart, Erlof't_203
Hayashi, Mizuho_266
Hayden, John_125
Hayden, Melissa_064
Hayes, Amanda_188
Haynes, Andrea_175
Hedde, Antje_022, 023
Heller, Steven_064
Henkels Gestaltet_052
Henley, Stuart_064
Henn, Oliver_231
Henss, Professor Roland_231
Herms, Ralf_225
Hersey, John_076
Hesse Designstudios_139
Hesse, Klaus_139
Hest & Kramer_257
Hickmann, Fons M._042, 210
Higashi, Keiko_151

Himmler, Helmut_236
HKF Film–und
Fernsehproduktion_039
Hodges, Drew_148, 156
Hodgson, Michael_083, 189
Hoebé, Henk_203
Hoffman, Mark_226
Hoffman, Susan_208
Holm Graphic Service_044
Holmquist, Holly_192
Hoppe, Ulrich_230
House of Naylor_144
Hudson's_048, 086
Hudson, John_277, 280, 288
Hunt, Karen Jean_158
Hunzinger Information AG_149
Hwang, Christina_209
Hyde, Deborah_133, 215
Hyogo, Shinji_266
I IBM_253
Ilić, Mirko_113, 211, 219
Illinois Arts Council_24
Imaginary Forces_190, 195, 201,
205, 209, 220, 226, 227
Independent Medien – Design_261
Infrarot GmbH_074
Inter Medium Institute Graduate
School_199
International Design Center_113
Iontef Type Foundry_299
Iontef, Yanek_299
Iorillo, Jeff_201
Issey Miyake_183
Ivex Packaging Corporation_174
J J. Walter Thompson_195
Jacks, James_227
Jackson, Frances_184
Jager Di Paola Kemp Design_055,
059, 136
Jager, Michael_055, 059, 136
Jakab, Mike_227
Jankens, Jeff_205
Janus Mutual Funds_201
Japan Bridge_198, 200
Japan Typography Association_075
Jarre, Kevin_227
JDP_068
Jennifer Sterling Design_030, 054,
066, 177
Jerde, Jennifer_192
Jet Tone Film Production_157
Joanie Bernstein, Art Rep_135
Joerg Bauer Design_224
Johann Jacobs Museum_143
Johnson & Wolverton_133, 208, 215
Johnson, Alicia_133, 215
Jones, Lillian_158
Jones, Todd ap_135
Josef, Arendas_178
Joseph, Douglas_069
Jung Dentaltechnik_070
Just Type Anything_182
just-type-anything.com_182
K Kajita, Azusa_123
Karlsson, Hjalti_194
Kartsotis, Kosta_168
Katona, Diti_169, 178
Kaye, Michael Ian_228
Kays, Adrian_195
Keiler & Company_080, 081
Kempf, Claudia_121
Kenny, Saffron_195, 205, 209, 217,
227
Kern, Geof_26
Keun, Eben_249

Kidd, Chip_010, 014, 024
Kimura, Masahiko_106
Kling, Jeff_208
Knaeble, Catherine_048, 086
Kobayashi, Akira_297
Kobayashi, Jane_240
Koch, Floridan_225
Koch, Nicole_210
Koch, Rafael_225
Kolomayets, Ivan_024
Kolsrud, Dan_217
Kompas Design_068
Kono, Carol_189
Konuma, Takashi_300
Kopald, Larry_234
Körner, Andreas_139
Körner, Peter_225
Kosem, Jim_179
Kotze, Steven_249
KPlant Co., Ltd._131
Kraus, Marcus_070
Krivanek, B.J._24, 158
Krueger, Kevin_162, 251
Kubota, Makota_254
Kunsthochschule Kassel_103
Küompel, Kristina_210
The Kuricorder Foundation_172
kurigami, kazumi_244
Kurylak, Lydia_024
Kusada, Yoshiko_115
Kusagaya Design, Inc._040, 134
Kusagaya, Takafumi_040, 134
Kwan, Godfrey_157
Kwan, Theresa_178
Kwong, Elaine_071
Lahti Polytechnic Institute
of Design_166
Lambert, Scott_069
Langdon, Karen_130
Lau, Grant_205
Laubhan, Lisa_195, 201
L Lauerman, Bailey_125
Layne, Heather_043
Ledoux, Patrice_226
Lee, Byron_064
Lehmann, Claus_074
Lehni, Urs_225
Leifer, Thomas_052, 149
Leinonen, Ritva_166
Leonhardt + Kern_224
Leslie Chan Design Co._060
A.M. Leslie_116
Libreria Giannino Stoppani_106
Lin, Kuan Ling_119
Lines, Edward, Jr._024
Linotype Library_309
Lippa Pearce Design_122, 255
Lippa, Domenic_122, 255
Little, Brown and Company_228
Ljungkvist, Laura_080
Lohmann, Stefan_210
Longhuest, Dan_242
Lopez, Ben_209, 227
Lopez, Chris_205, 209
Lothar Bertrams_072
Luminet, Jean Pierre_222
Lundy, Clare_255
M M.A.D._202
Mabry, Michael_202
Macau Designers Association_060
Machó, Rafael_201
Maclean, Douglas_259
Madeira, Paul_220
Maisey, Oliver_212
Maksimovic & Partners_138

Maksimovic, Ivica_138
Malone, Greg Paul_209
Man, Phil_205, 220, 226
Mantzaris, Chris_201
Marandi, Sara_220
Marquis, Matthew_213
Marshall Field's_048, 086
Martin, Fletcher_128
Marzaroli, Vanessa_213
Maschmann, Werner_103
Massard, Rymn_228
The Masters_248
Mathews, Su_145
Mattila, Kurt_220, 226
McCann Erickson_188
McCarr, Casey_175
McGillan, Richard_255
McManus, Brenda_170
MCS Design_104
Meave, Gabriel Martinez_294, 302
Meier, Hans Eduard_309
Melcher, Gordon_234
Melichar, Uwe_039
Merrifield, Brian_212
Merrill Lynch_195
MetaDesign_184
Metropolis_067, 102
Meyer, Constantin_103
MGM Grand_241
Michael Conrad & Leo Burnett_236
Michel, Olivier_222
Mike Salisbury LLC_241
Miller, J. Abbott_243
Milly Films_053
Mirko Ilić Corp._113, 219
Miura, Iwao_266
Miyajima, Takafumi_040
Modern Dog Design Co._107
Moed, Andrea_064
Moehler, Michelle_196
Mohawk Paper Mills_064
Molloy, Jack_135
Morioka, Adams_202
Morrison, Tim_247
Moser, Horst _261
Mott, Emily_064
Mucca Design Corporation_051
Müller, Sabine_203
Municipality of Pesaro_262
Murphy Design_179
Murphy, Mark_179
Mutert, Simone_120
Mycielski, Dominik_185
N N • G., Inc._244
Naerheim, Tor_241
Nagai, Hiroaki_244
Nakajima Design_204
Nakajima, Hideki_204
Nakasuji, Osamu_088
Namaye, Darren_126, 127, 163
Napp, Peter_170
Nash, Mitch_107
Nebraska Art Association_125
Neil Leifer_211
Nelson, Sarah_135, 159
Nenye, Sakari_166
Nesnadny + Schwartz_196
Nesnadny, Joyce_196
New Fonts_306
New York University_238
New Zealand Symphony
Orchestra_212
Niemann, Carolin_139
Niemann, Christoph_064
Nifuji, Masakazu_244

Nimbus Design_181
Nishi, Katsunori_117, 160, 252
Nix, Charles_306
Nogami Design Office_065, 075
Nogami, Shuichi_065, 075
Nowak, Stefan_185
Nuforia, Inc._126, 127, 163

O O'Donnel, Aaron_259
O'Neil, Chris_188
Oechtering, Lisa Schulze_070
Oh Boy, A Design Company_043, 197
Okumura, Akio_151, 198, 199, 200
Olan, Anita_205, 226
Olsen, Erik_077
Olsen, Jon_076, 193
Olsen, Peter_145
Onward Kashiyama Co., Ltd._244
Orange Juice Design_246, 249
Otto, Sue_061
Oxygen Design_300

P Packaging Create Inc._198, 199, 200
Padilla, Robert_051
Paffrath, Johannes_225
Panke, Eric_081
ParaType_288, 301, 303
Parker, Kingsley_118
Parkinson, John_220
Parr, Martin_22
Parsons, Tucker_228
The Partners Film Company_084, 096
Pask, Guy_259
Pastis Restaurant_051
Patrignani, Massimiliano_262
Paul Shaw/Letter Design_141
Pearce, Harry_122
Peila, Joe_055, 136, 208
Pemrick, Lisa_037, 062, 105, 155, 171
Penn State School of Visual Arts_085
Pentagram_064, 067, 098, 102, 145, 235, 243
Peon, Monica_146
Perkin, Cynthia_024
Pesce, Giorgio_079, 129, 161
Peter Bain Design_141
Petersen, Jeff Kurt_158
Petersen, Michael_057
Peterson & Company_050
Petrich, Christina_207
Petrick Design_174
Petrick, Robert_174
Ph.D_083, 189
Pham, Benjamin_254
Phelps, Bill_137
Philadelphia College of Textiles & Science_082
Photonica USA_133, 215
Picasso, Dan_135
Piercy, Clive_083, 189
Piper-Hauswirth, Todd_062, 155
Plunkert, David_109, 187
Pluto_193
Poletto, Maurizio_225
Poof_239
Porchez, Jean-François_298
Pouchet, Denise_226
Poulin, L. Richard_115
Powell, Kerrie_235
Powers, Marion English_180, 223
Pregler, Debra_220
Pro Helvetica, Art Council of Switzerland_246
319 Probst, Ken_137
PRoGRESS bureau of design_234
The Progressive Corporation_196

Push_191
Pylypczak, John_169, 178
Q Qualcomm_205
R +rosebud_225
Radcliffe, Mark_217
Rädeker, Jochen_218
Randall, Andrew_193
Ray, Scott_050
Razorfish_213
Reebok International, Ltd._126, 127
Reichelt, Sibylle_103
RGP Paris_222
Rhee, JoJo_145
Richardson, Nigel_212
Richardson, Terry_22
Rigsby Design_012
Rigsby, Lana_012, 016, 026, 027
Ritter, Dave_253
Roat, Rich_064
Rob Weisbach Books_140
Roberson, Kevin_124, 137
Robert McDougall Art Gallery_259
Roberts, Karla_024
Robertson-Ceco Corporation_197
Robledo, Maria_064
Rock Hong Kong Company Limited_071
rockin'on inc._266
Rodgers Litho_038
Rodriguez, Susana_253
Rolf, Richard_144
Rollins, Henry_195
Römerturm Feinpapiere_230
Rosenfield, Tom_201
Ruby in the Soda_214
Rusoff, Lance_061
Rutgers University—Newark_170
S "S" Wonderland Co., Ltd._131
Saatchi & Saatchi Advertising_209, 212
Safayev, Tagir_303
Sagmeister Inc._194, 237, 265
Sagmeister, Stefan_194, 237, 265
Sahre, Paul_140
Salanitro, David_043, 197
Salisbury, Mike_241
Saltz, Ina_012, 016, 028
Salvas, Justin_164
Samata, Greg_162
Samata, Pat_251
SamataMason_162, 251
Sandstrom Design_193
Sandstrom, Steve_076, 087, 193
Sarfati, Frank_053
Sato, Takahito_123
Sayuri Studio_183
Schecter, Dana_188
Schemmrich_139
Scher, Paula_067, 102
Schierlitz, Tom_265
Schindler, Heribert_230
Schlatter, Robert_130, 137
Schlichting, Sandra_052
Schmauder, Claudia_143
Schmidt, Katrin_039
Schmidt, Stefan_022
Schneider, Werner_28, 29
Scholing, Alex_206
School of Visual Arts_111, 114, 115, 119, 164, 165
Schrebetz-Skyba, Lenaa_24
Schreiber, Curtis_128, 253
Schulte, Jason_037, 062, 171
Schwartz, Mark_196
Scorsone, Joe_036, 153
Scorsone/Drueding_036, 153

Scricco, Mike_080, 081
Seeger, Hans_253
Sega Dreamcast_190
Segura Inc._058, 216
Segura, Carlos_058, 216
Seibold, J. Otto_108
Seki, Hiroaki_244
Sekigushi, Miki_040
Sekikawa, Hideyuki_172
Shaw, Paul_141
Shields, David_233
Shift_256
Shikano, Atsushi_266
Shinnoske Inc._088
Shoji, Sayuri_183
Shourie, Rishi_190
Shrimpf, David_239
Shya, Wing_071, 157
Shya-la-la Workshop Ltd._071, 157
Sierman, Gijs_229
[sign*]_053, 150
Sikora, Steven_257
Simmons, Todd_130
Sinkinson, Topher_133, 215
Slaughter Hanson_180, 223
Slaughter, Terry_180
Slavin, Neal_064
Slimbach, Robert_305
Smith, Chuck_239
Smith, David_167
Socio X_010
Sommers, Stephen_227
Sommerville, James_012, 016, 030
Sommese Design_085
Sommese, Lanny_085
Sonnoli, Leonardo_262, 267
Sorren, Joe_135
Soterolopis, Connie_048, 086
Spicers Paper Inc._069
Spike Networks_054
Spinal Diagnostics and Treatment Center_077
Spot Design_148, 156
Spotco._148, 156
Springer & Jacoby_022, 023, 207
SPUR Design LLC_109, 187
Stampley, Susie_168, 175
Starr, Sarah_208
Steele, Casey_213
Steinlicht, David_044
Sténuit, Oliver_053
Stephens, Christine_256
Stephens, Jeff_174
Sterling, Jennifer_030, 031, 054, 066, 177, 202
Stichting Educatieve Omroep Teleac/NOT_167
Stojanovi'c, Slavimir_068
Stoller, Dani_209
Stone, JoAnn_145
Štorm Type Foundry_284
Štorm, František_284
Strategy Advertising & Design_259
strichpunkt_218
Strike Co., Ltd._123
Stuart, Glenda_260
Studio Bau Winkel_203
Studio d Design_038, 044, 047, 105
Studio Dumbar_146, 203
Studio Hans Verlaat_203
Studio Henk Hoebé_203
Studley, Vance_232
Stürzebecher, Jörg_103
Sudheim, Alex_249
Suffness, Dorit_050

Sugisaki, Shinnoske _088
Superstudios_206
Swensen, Bob_220, 226
Swift, Elvis_048, 086, 135
T Takashimaya New York_026, 142
Takechi, Jun_172, 214
Takeo, Inc._040
Tamás, Veress_049
Tan, Winnie_181
Tanaka, Katsuyuki_131
Tanaka, Rikiya_266
Tankard, Jeremy_295
Tanner, Ellen_175
TBA+D_063
Tel Design_203
Tepper, Arielle_156
Teufel, Phillip_185
TGV Inc._134
Thares, Scott_257
Thaw, Jacqueline_064
Théâtre Arsenic_079, 129, 161
Thienhaus, Régino_121
Thijssen, André_167
Think New Ideas_234
Thorburn, Bill_239
Tide_209
Tielmann, Judith_149
Tilin, Andrew_064
Time Hotel_219
Timpa, Maureen_220
Tinkel, Kathleen_277, 280, 290
Todd, Mark_233
Toensmann, Christian_112
Tojuso Center_088
Tokimoto, Tomohiro_199
Tollifson, Craig_213
Tolo, Jennifer_192
Tony Stone_116
Tower Records Inc._117
Tracy Chaney_043
Travel Channel_213
Treder, Judith_236
Trendbüro B.K.W._121
Truschkowski, Maike_103
Tsukada, Minao_123
Tsukamoto, Akihiko_045, 173
Tucker, Eric_069
Tulea Art Directors Club_038
Turkalo, Sinovi_024
Twin-Eight Co., Ltd._045, 173
Twombly, Carol_305
Type Behaviour and Kitsch Publishing_056
Typographic Circle_255
U Uebele, Andreas_072
UNA_167, 203
Unicef_106
Universal_227
University for Applied Science, Bielefeld_121
University of Illinois_078
Uno, Koremasa_266
Unruh, Jack_080
Urban Outfitters_061
Utterback, Camille_238
V Vagnoni, Anthony_012, 016, 032
Van Audenhaege, Joël_053
van Dÿk, Bob_146
Van Gastel, Mikon_190, 195, 217, 220
van Lindonk Special Projects_229
van Lindonk, Peter_229
Van Winkle, Jennifer_24
Vanderbyl, Michael_202

Veljovi'c, Jovica_308
Verdaguet, Raymond_081
Verhoorn, Kara_209
Verlaat, Hans_203
Versorgungs – und Verkehrsgesellschaft Saarbruecken_138
Victore, James_111, 202
Vincent, Scott_205
Vineyard, John_175
Virtual Telemetrix_202
Voelker, Jean Ulysses_231
von Alvensleben, Christian_139
Vorbeck, Siri_210
Vorm Vijk_203
Vosloo, Brode_246, 249
VSA Partners_057, 128, 253
W Wagenhofer, Konstanze_225
Wagner, Valerie_164
Walker, Garth_249
Wallace, Paula_175
Wang, Mike_253
Wangsillapakun, Teeranop_058, 216
Wargin, Christopher_234
Warlich Druck, Meckenheim_046
WBMG, Inc._211
Webb, Jason_201, 217
Weber, Uli_224
Weiler, Jan_230
Weitz, Carter_125
Wenzel, Martin_307
Werner Design Werks, Inc._135, 159
Werner, Sharon_135, 159
White Gas_233
Why Not Associates_010
Wieden & Kennedy_208
Wijaya, Effendy_165
Wild, Lorraine_064
Wilkens, Dann_190
Williams, Allison_026, 142, 147
Williams, J.P._026, 142, 147
Williams, Jeff_208
Williams, Kathleen_208
Williamson Printing Corporation_047, 105
Wimmer, Hunter L._197
Wink_191
Winkel, Bau_203
Wippermann, Prof. Peter_121
Wohlhüter, Marcus_225
Wolf, Karl_086
Wolverton, Hal_208
Wong, Nelson_183
Wongsunkakon, Anuthin_056, 186
Woodtli, Martin_265
Y Yale School of Architecture_235
Yang, James_080
Yefimov, Vladimir_288
Yomiko Advertising Inc._244
Yoon, Danny_205, 209, 220, 227
yosho.com_058, 216
Young & Rubicam_012
Z Zareba, Justyna_111
Zeebelt Theatre_146
zefa visual media_210
Zhang, Stephen_168, 175
Zhukov, Maxim_273
Zsigmond, Vilmos, ASC_226
Zuan Club_045, 173

TDC 46
TDC² 2000

TDC 46 CHAIR

SUSAN COTLER-BLOCK
FASHION INSTITUTE OF TECHNOLOGY

TDC 46 JURY

BRIGETTE DESOCIO, SOHO X
DAVID ELLIS, WHY NOT ASSOCIATES
CHIP KIDD, CHIP KIDD DESIGN
LANA RIGSBY, RIGSBY DESIGN
INA SALTZ, GOLF MAGAZINE
JAMES SOMMERVILLE, ATTIK
ANTHONY VAGNONI, YOUNG & RUBICAM

TDC² 2000 CHAIR

MAXIM ZHUKOV
UNITED NATIONS

TDC² 2000 JURY

MATTHEW CARTER, CARTER & CONE TYPE INC.
BARRY DECK
JOHN HUDSON, TIRO TYPEWORKS
KATHLEEN TINKEL